EBURY PRESS

ON BEAUTY

Prathyush Parasuraman holds a BA in economics and South Asian studies from the University of California, Berkeley. He is passionate about pedagogy, research, policy, film, literature and economic theory. A cultural critic and journalist, Prathyush has worked as a film critic with Film Companion for five years.

On Beauty

THE CINEMA OF SANJAY LEELA BHANSALI

Prathyush Parasuraman

EBURY PRESS

An imprint of Penguin Random House

EBURY PRESS

Ebury Press is an imprint of the Penguin Random House group of companies whose addresses can be found at global.penguinrandomhouse.com

Published by Penguin Random House India Pvt. Ltd
4th Floor, Capital Tower 1, MG Road,
Gurugram 122 002, Haryana, India

Penguin Random House India

First published in Ebury Press by Penguin Random House India 2024

10 9 8 7 6 5 4 3 2 1

ISBN 9780143465980

Typeset in Sabon LT Std by Manipal Technologies Limited, Manipal

www.penguin.co.in

For Az,
who taught me to separate the beautiful
from the sublime

'I'm enmeshed sufficiently
In the physical
to reel drunkenly before
holy gestures.'

—'Should One Come To Me',
Gieve Patel, poet and playwright

'For this is the right way to proceed or to let yourself be led in matters of love: Start from an individual expression or form of beauty. Climb higher and higher for the sake of that beauty, as though climbing the steps of a ladder. Ascend from the first to the next, and then to all forms of beauty. From beautiful forms, go on to beautiful practices and conduct. From there, continue to the study of beauty until you arrive at that knowledge that is of nothing else but pure beauty. And that is where you will finally recognize and know beauty itself.'

—Diotima, according to Socrates in
Plato's Symposium, c. 380 BCE

'Beauty cannot be an expression of thought.'

—Jiddu Krishnamurti,
philosopher and orator

Contents

Introduction

The Limits of Beauty

In November 2007, two days before the release of *Saawariya*, director Sanjay Leela Bhansali's fifth film, the executives of Sony Pictures Entertainment, the producer of the magnum opus, were hauled into a screening room. This would be the first time they were going to see the film—which Bhansali had been nursing, editing and tinkering with, unwilling to let it rip into the world, fiercely guarding it from everyone's gaze, even that of the studio head.

Based on Fyodor Dostoevsky's short story 'White Nights', *Saawariya* was crafted and announced as a milestone film, made at a then-egregious, now-mainstream budget of ₹35–50 crore, backed by Sony, which became the first Hollywood studio to produce an Indian film.

With *Saawariya*, Sonam Kapoor and Ranbir Kapoor, Bombay cinema royalty—she, the daughter of Anil Kapoor, a first-generation star of the 1980s and '90s, and he, the son of Rishi Kapoor, a third-generation star of the

1970s and '80s—were making their debut together. No budget spared, the nepo-kids were flown across the country to promote them, both individually and together, alongside the film. Around the same time, *Vogue* magazine made landfall on the subcontinent with a gonging launch, which included a 'Bollywood Dreams' photo essay, featuring the sets of the film, the actors and Bhansali himself. *Saawariya* was set to release at the same time as the Shah Rukh Khan-starrer *Om Shanti Om*, a meta blitzkrieg offensive of charm and nostalgia, and so the buzz, the anxiety, was all the more deafening.

Sony had been marketing the film solely on the basis of the screenplay and the trailer—which itself was delivered weeks after the decided-upon deadline, much to the frustration of the studio. The film was a black hole for all intents and purposes. No one had any idea how the film in its entirety looked, what its narrative shape or its aesthetic gloss felt like when watched end to end, how the saturated blues of the film would leak or linger in the viewer's mind, and how the stretching of time across four nights would disturb or dry over the matrix of consciousness. Uday Singh, who was the managing director of Sony at the time, noted, 'It was a bubble you had to believe in.'[1]

That bubble burst.

As the executives settled in to watch the film, panic struck. The film felt dull, bleak and uninteresting. It was too late for course corrections. Days later, on 9 November 2007, when the film released, their intuition was confirmed. *Saawariya* tanked, both critically and commercially. The reviews were blistering, some calling it 'contrived and fake'[2], and the public rejection almost sulphurous. People wondered if Bhansali, the artist who was floating high after the deafening success of his previous two films—*Devdas* (2002), which premiered at the Cannes Film Festival, and *Black* (2005), which was, at that time, the most-awarded film at the Filmfare Awards—had lost it. Bathed in shades of blue, *Saawariya* was the first film he shot entirely indoors. His '*khwabon ka sheher*', his city of dreams, which he erected on the outskirts of Mumbai, was considered too beautiful, too indulgent, too artificial.

The film made Rs 11 crore in the opening weekend, and four more through the month, unable to break even. *Saawariya,* the first Hindi film to carry the logo of Columbia-Tristar—the Sony division that produced the film—would also be the reason they nearly shut down here,[3] re-evaluating their India strategy.[4] The executives were called to New York to explain the disaster. Film award shows turned *Saawariya* into the punchline of their many grating, some grinning, punches. There was a grim relish in this failure, burnished by the parallel runaway success of *Om Shanti Om*. Bhansali retreated to Paris, where he would direct an opera.

It is here that I want to begin my monograph. A failure so humiliating, so serrated, that it exposed the fault lines of cinema and criticism itself.

There is this conservative belief that a film must merely tell a story—where the script should be tight, the attention must be laser-sharp, distilled and nothing, not even the world in which the story unfolds, should distract you from the story itself. To be lean, taut, clear and smooth.

Then, there is the collective filmography of writer, director, editor, music composer and choreographer Sanjay Leela Bhansali: a two-and-a-half-decade exercise in swooning beauty and blinding artifice—in staining a movie with so many, so much music that sometimes the story collapses under the weight of its gilded filaments and filigrees. It is in the rubble of that collapse where we can find his cinema.

In films, beauty matters. In his films, *only* beauty matters. The conventional characterization of his films goes something like this: At his best, he is able to pulse the film's beauty with an emotional pungence, a citric gash that makes you sit up and take notice; at his worst, there is only beauty. *Saawariya* tumbled squarely into the latter category.

This characterization—a rather lazy one—brings up the fundamental philosophical question of beauty. If beauty does not move you, if it does not quake your sense of space, time and being, but merely exists outside of you, leaving you unmoved as it drones over a film screen, is it still beauty?

Isn't beauty that *through* which the self throbs, as opposed to being something outside of the self that merely needs nodding at? Can you, then, watch a film, call it beautiful, and yet find it boring, affectless or tiring? To put it simply, can a dull thing be beautiful?

I have not been able to square how critics and crowds walked out of *Saawariya*, confidently calling every frame of the film a painting, appreciating the painstaking eye that produced it, and yet dismissing the film, nonetheless. What does this say about how shallow, how distant, how anaesthetic our ideas of 'beauty' are? Or just how dismissively and casually we use the word 'beauty'? Or for that matter, how we conceive of 'goodness' and 'beauty' with respect to cinema.

It is my belief that beauty, necessarily, requires submission. The beauty of Bhansali's films, necessarily, requires submission. That dull things can be beautiful, but if the beauty were true, whole and consummate, that dullness would never be apparent, merely a soft itch to be scratched away; that dullness itself would be transformed into something else, something radiant by being beautiful. Is that not why we are so suspicious of beauty—of how it derails our consciousness? And is that not why we hoist our guards in the company of beauty—what are you masking, we ask the beautiful thing? And is that not also how we turn from aesthetes to sceptics, forcing every impulse to be analysed under the harsh light of reason?

Those critical of his films, of his style, of the operatic intensity, the exaggerated overtures, the emotional violence, the careful compositions, the symmetric despair, are not critical of him as much as they are airing their inability to submit. What lurks behind this inability, this scepticism, this distance?

Conversely, what explains the rapt immediacy of submission, the uncritical embrace of his grand madness? Why do Bhansali's images hold such a complicated, hypnotic power? It is this singular question that animates this monograph.

Born on 24 February 1963 to a family barely making ends meet amidst the entrepreneurial fumes of Gujarati migrants, in a chawl in South Bombay at the corner of Nal Bazar and Bhuleshwar, Sanjay Leela Bhansali grew up lonely, sharing a tight space with his sister and parents.

'All my early impressions are of prostitutes hanging around with clients and vivid colours . . . there were eight movie theatres on the lane to school. I'd watch strange films and stare at the strange posters. The prostitutes would bring their clients to the halls, and we'd watch the films, half-wondering what they were doing in the back. The theatres of South Mumbai were wonderful. The clean windows, the air conditioning, Apsara theatre with its art deco. It was like a dream world. A palace,' Bhansali reminisced in an interview with writer Nisha Susan.[5]

His father, Navin Bhansali, though an unsuccessful film producer, made sure cinema swaddled, surrounded and seduced him. With his father, Sanjay watched *Mughal-e-Azam* (1960) eighteen times in the theatre. When Navin's films finished shooting, trunks of costume and make-up would be stored at their house, keeping Sanjay company. Sometimes, Navin would take Sanjay with him to film shoots. An early cabaret shoot that Sanjay saw as a child seared into his mind; the confected, airtight perfection of a film set would sow the seed of shooting within the controlled beauty of a studio.

When Susan asked Bhansali about his first memory, the cabaret shoot was what he returned to.

> 'I think I was four. My father took me along to a studio where he was meeting a friend. He asked me to sit quietly in a corner of the set and went off. I was most comfortable. I looked at the catwalks. What my father didn't realize was that a cabaret was being shot. A girl walked in and removed the shawl around her. She was wearing a skimpy, off-white dress. She had to jump over a half-naked man, who was lying on a bed and throw an apple at him. They did it again, and then they did it again. I was completely hypnotized. She was wearing horns. It was bizarre. Then my father came and took

> me away. As I talk about it, it seems more bizarre. But it is my most vivid impression of beauty. It seduced me immediately.'

Not very bright in school, not very sociable at home, he would spend time listening to the radio, watching his mother crack open the day by dancing to songs that would crackle from the stereo. He got through the Film and Television Institute of India, Pune on his second attempt, and studied editing. Directors like Sriram Raghavan and Rajkumar Hirani lived on the same floor as him—but Bhansali kept to himself. Although he graduated, he was unable to complete his diploma film because he was thrown out due to differences with the institute director. He took the matter to court and lost.

His sister, Bela Segal, who was working with Vidhu Vinod Chopra on *Parinda* (1989) at the time, introduced him to the director. And so began Bhansali's career directing the songs in *Parinda* and, later, *1942: A Love Story* (1994). A trained Odissi dancer, back then, he thought his path was meandering towards becoming a choreographer. The penchant for stylizing, for creating enduring visuals, for elevating a story *through* the visuals of dance, was clear.

That he became a director *through* dance is unsurprising. It was how he engaged with Hindi cinema. In Nasreen Munni Kabir's *Bollywood: The Indian Cinema Story*, he notes, 'My passion was not to go and see a movie; my passion was to see how Helen danced in a film. How did they shoot Vyjayantimala [sic] or Waheeda Rehman as they danced?'

This is what a musical dance sequence does to cinema—it acts *upon* it, it energizes it, it scrapes against it, it alchemizes it; they can emerge uneasily, abruptly from a scene, pushing the film in directions that did not feel possible earlier. These are not just distinct spaces for fabulation, though they are that, too. In anticipation of these moments, sometimes, the movie throbs. The aftershocks last till scenes after. It is the mud-pit of joy, sex, sensuality and *nakhra*—that excessive blend of all things pleasurable and expressive.

When you think of *1942: A Love Story*, one of the first images that flash, perhaps, is that of Manisha Koirala in flowing white, her dupatta woven out of silken air, and cinematographer Binod Pradhan's dreamy halo lighting of the song 'Kuch Na Kaho'. A white so scrubbed and polished, emitting light itself, a flush of photons. The whole musical sequence, directed by Bhansali, a romantic mush, takes place on the stage of an auditorium, a modest, artificial setting, a modesty and artifice that has never pressed pause on his exploding imagination.

Much later, in his sixth film *Guzaarish* (2010), that trails Ethan Mascarenhas (played by Hrithik Roshan), a magician who, after an injury, becomes paraplegic and demands the right for euthanasia, Bhansali would, similarly, sculpt an entire dance sequence—'Jaane Kiske Khwaab', a flashback—on a stage. Since Ethan is a magician, Bhansali made conical beams of light look like inclines from whose edges Ethan can slide up and down, and a transparent ball becomes a prop over which his body contorts only to become a supple, fragile bubble that pops into glittering confetti. While his penchant for maximalism, for picturizing music with breathtaking scale and precision, would push his name to the forefront of image-making in Indian cinema, it is this capacity to mount entire songs around modest sets—sometimes a stage, sometimes a bed ('Ang Laga De', *Ram-Leela*), sometimes a wall ('Thode Badmaash', *Saawariya*), sometimes the back seat of a car ('Meri Jaan', *Gangubai Kathiawadi*)—that would often go unremarked.

To see how 'Kuch Na Kaho' became 'Jaane Kiske Khwaab', over a period of sixteen years, is to see a filmography sediment with fury, intensity and most apparently, scale. Every Bhansali film challenges what you think a Bhansali film is. What is constant is beauty. What keeps increasing is sweep. What refuses to die, despite failure, despite humiliation, is a reckless confidence.

There is a deeper question here, however. What is it about these songs that lingers like strong perfume—is it the beauty or is it the love between characters, the erupting joy that girds the song, providing an excuse for the beauty? And in Bhansali's artistry, does the former come at the expense of the latter?

If, as *New Yorker* critic Richard Brody writes, more than 'telling a story, shaping performances, or conveying emotions, the art of directing is creating a unified spectrum of experience', and that '[a] good director is like a powerful magnetic field whose presence orients the film's many elements, from the big ideas to the fine details, to form a double-sided reflection of the world at large and of the filmmaker's inner world,'[6] with what has Bhansali magnetized his cinema?

He made his feature film debut in 1996 with *Khamoshi: The Musical*, a sombre film about the musical daughter of deaf-and-mute parents, set in Goa. A commercial failure, he changed gears subsequently, flushing his palette with colour, texture, rage and drama that is loud, brash and articulate with *Hum Dil De Chuke Sanam* (1998), set in Gujarat and Italy—Budapest, actually, that he passed for Italy—and *Devdas* (2002), set in his gilded version of feudal Bengal and Banaras—a set, actually, that he passed for Bengal and Banaras. He turned his back to colour with the melancholic *Black* (2005), *Saawariya* (2007), and *Guzaarish* (2010), only to find himself back in the disorienting slap of *gulaal* in *Ram-Leela* (2013), *Bajirao Mastani* (2015) and *Padmaavat* (2018). His latest feature film *Gangubai Kathiawadi* (2022) marked a return to the penumbraless gash of white playing with its various shades, its different textures, its distinct silhouettes. From here, he made a swerve into long-form storytelling with *Heeramandi* (2024), expressing the preoccupations that have haunted him for decades—the maximalist courtesan figure, the wretched woman whose dignity is her wretchedness—with a new vocabulary of not just style, but also storytelling. Where once he would lavish his attention, as both director and editor, on a song by never allowing your attention to waver away from the affect emanating like vapour from the stilled storytelling for the entire duration of the performance, with *Heeramandi* he shows a comfort with cutting away from the mujra, to return to it, as though the song has lost its centrality, as though he succumbed to the belief that music is not essence but embellishment.

Even as his filmography has warped and wefted through the colour palette (the white film, the red film, the gray film, the blue—no, the *indigo* film), you can sense a growing body of work that is congealing on a 'style': a '*chhaap*' that is distinctive.

One element of this 'style' is his thematic obsession with emotional violence. Another is his aesthetic lunge towards the 'top shot'. Then, there is his technical preference for longer shots, especially in dances or emotional sequences that require you to notice the twitch of the eyebrows, the teardrop forming and slipping down the cheek, the saliva collecting at the edge of the mouth, and the flare of the eyes.

Characters will laugh and cry as though the two were extensions of the same feeling. So, when Gulab (Rani Mukerji), the sex worker in *Saawariya* speaks to Ranbir Raj (Ranbir Kapoor), the wanderer who tripped and fell into this town, of how, as babies they wept through the night, with neither their mothers who were busy selling their bodies, nor any fairy coming to coax them, she is laughing at her pathetic fate, but there is a glaze of wetness on her eyes. Later, Ranbir tells his mysterious lover, Sakina (Sonam Kapoor), '*Aapki hasi mein bhi abhi thodi sadness baqi hai*,'—in your laugh, there is a trace of sadness left. Such is the emotional *dhoop-chhaon* of the characters, turning this way and that, which Bhansali sketches out of pathos, beauty, and an abrasive longing. This instability is produced by the intention of the director, the craft of the actor, but also the choice of the editor—to allow the camera to let this fragility brew without condensing it, cutting from it, letting the eyes hold the glaze of glycerine.

When the transition was made from film to digital, film-makers, suddenly unencumbered by the budgeted number of reels, began to shoot extensively, taking multiple takes from multiple angles, editing it into a quicker, slicker switcheroo of a scene. Not Bhansali. For him, the dynamism of a dance sequence comes not from the quick-footed edit but the dance itself, allowing each choreographed gesture to be shown, germinating from nothingness to its final pose without the charismatic but distracting cinematic cut. What the long shot—as opposed to long 'take', which focuses on the many different stabs the filmmaker takes to capture a moment, with 'shot' implying the final one that we see stitched onto the screen—also does is that it allows you to sit with a moment, breathe it in, allowing yourself to be sucked into its beauty, without the strobe-light-like scissoring which stuns you into paying attention.

That Bhansali edits most of his films, and that he thinks like an editor while shooting as a director, allows him more control over the duration of scenes, the location of a cut, the decision to switch perspective and direction. When watching other films, notice when a shot begins and when it ends, and count the lapsed time on your fingers. Often, one hand would suffice. It is the kind of impatient editing that we have absorbed as our fractured experience of cinema, of time within the screen. Bhansali's films offer the possibility of rediscovering patience, of inhabiting time on-screen the way we brush against it in life.

~

When I say that in Bhansali's films, only beauty matters, I am being extremely literal, not given to brash exaggeration or a grand gesture to dizzy you with the sweeping stance of my opinion.

Let me clarify this controversial pose with a controversy, looking at how the politics in his films have been discussed, and how those who have criticized Bhansali's art for being conservative or Islamophobic or patriarchal often see his penchant for beauty in opposition to their liberal political beliefs for dignity and freedom.

In my reading of his films, politics seems so beyond his viewfinder, sometimes a political reading or reaction to his films feels odd. Odd, not because it isn't valid or needed or, but because it is trying to give a film a political intention where none seems to exist—like trying to yank debris out of a vacuum or meaning out of beauty. The point of beauty is not to furnish meaning. Why forage for it, then?

Let us turn our gaze to *Padmaavat* (2018), his ninth and most expensive film based on the sixteenth-century epic poem by Malik Muhammad Jayasi. Set in the twelfth century, the film retells the folk legend of Rani Padmavati (Deepika Padukone), who, after the death of her husband, the Rajput king Ratan Singh (Shahid Kapoor) by the Delhi Sultan Alauddin Khilji (Ranveer Singh), decides to immolate herself so that Khilji never gets to possess her. The idea of self-immolation, sati or *jauhar*, a brutal act of a woman giving up her life to uphold a patriarchal standard of dignity and purity—to be untouched by the enemy—is an archaic idea that Bhansali had decided to rouge and razz with beauty.

In the climax, a sea of women, dressed in crimson—children, aged, pregnant, everyone—run into a growling, simmering, fort-high, embering, computer-generated fire to commit jauhar, a crescendo, collective suicide, propelled by a haunting score and a strident slow motion that teases tension, allowing each flutter of the fabric to feel final. And it is precisely in the almost surreal beauty of the brutality, the artificiality of the fire itself, that the brutality is never allowed to state itself. Like watching women run into rust yellow pixels, the violence remains this ether-like idea.

This seems to be how he treats every situation. Often it is difficult to know if what we are submitting to is the emotional crust of the situation or its molten beauty. Even to this day, when Paro (Aishwarya Rai Bachchan) runs towards her lover, a dying Devdas (Shah Rukh Khan) at the end of *Devdas*, Bhansali's third and most celebrated film, a slow-motion that is punched by Paro's screeching, by the tension of the moment, her sari unfurling and like a white wave sculpted by the air, hovering, it is impossible to not be pounded into gooseflesh.

When you try to locate the source of this reaction, to psychologize this goose-fleshing, it is impossible to know if it is rooted in the emotional reach of the scene or the dramatic pyrotechnics of Bhansali's cinema or Monty Sharma's wailing score. It could be all three, of course. But more and more it seems, to me, that Bhansali's beauty is like a stain on a shirt. It is not like the shirt doesn't exist, it is just that your attention is always directed towards, hypnotized by, the stain.

So, it seemed impossible to see the moment in *Padmaavat* as one of horror, of feminism's dying, sighing breath, because Bhansali frames it as beauty, as awe, as a spectacle, as a gleaming image to end his film with. When, in an open letter, actress and activist Swara Bhaskar emphatically noted, 'Women have the right to live, despite being raped sir . . . Women are not only walking talking vaginas,'[7] it felt like the criticism was talking at cross-purposes with his cinema. That climax was never about women. It was about beauty.

This aestheticizing of everything—femininity, religion, trauma, history, desire—with a reckless irreverence towards 'reality', 'realism', 'the present condition' has produced his increasingly vacuum-sealed worlds. To criticize this escapism, however defensible, is an increasingly shrill and dull stroking of the chin, hand on the hip. There is a reason his films feel 'timeless', for by escaping the grounding demands of time and place, they escape the moral demands of that time and place, too.

Similarly, his treatment of Alauddin Khilji in *Padmaavat* as this monstrous, evil, sexualized beast who wants to possess Rani Padmavati, has been read as a rewriting of history, imposing present-day phobias and the trenchant representation of the Muslim as someone with an irresistible, irrepressible appetite, on the past. But the film, based on a folk tale, was never about history. It was about beauty.

For all my grumbling, my belief that his films are politically amphibious, you will point me in the direction of Bhansali giving, in a rare instance, a glimpse of his political proclivities. Here is Bhansali on Modi, the Prime Minister of India, who has reportedly brought to the surface, confidently, many of the xenophobic, Islamophobic tendencies that have always been simmering among us, 'I like the fact that he has something to say and something to achieve and a practical agenda to follow. I need to be inspired. I need to follow you. I think he is astute and that is important for a leader. The ability to have people follow you is important. Charisma is important.'[8]

With this quote floating about in your head, you must be asking me, can we not, then, extricate from Khilji's demonization—a character—Bhansali's demonization of the Muslim—an identity?

But what if you place this quote against a brief, sympathetic nod to Nehru in *Gangubai Kathiawadi*?

Or even this dialogue from the film, taken from Sahir Ludhianvi's lyrics for *Pyaasa*, '*Madad chahti hai, ye Hawwa ki beti, Yashoda ki hum-jins, Radha ki beti, Payambar ki ummat, Zulaikhan ki beti, Jinhen naaz hai Hind par woh kahan hai*', bringing in Hindu, Islamic, Christian and Jewish characters into a plea? What do you make of that stately, kind, what Bhansali called 'astute', representation of our first Prime Minister? Or the rousing monologue on secularism and how religion has never chosen a colour in *Bajirao Mastani*? What about the villainization of the Brahmins as a community in that film?

For all the accusations of Islamophobia, there seems no mention of how in *Saawariya*, Urdu words like 'jaan' are calligraphed with Mumtaz Mahal portraits and Lakshmi murals painted in shades borrowed from Monet's palette. The Ganga–Jamuna *tehzeeb* with a Hindu man pursuing a Muslim woman in *Saawariya* and *Bajirao Mastani*, or a Muslim man pursuing a Hindu woman in *Gangubai Kathiawadi*, can be read into as a progressive screech, but I believe these, too, are dull, decrepit readings, ignoring the surface to revel in something else, something easier—intended or constructed.

In his films, the subtext—that is, the discourse and material *under* the text, like hidden meanings, embedded metaphors, easter eggs—and the paratext—that is, the discourse and material *around* the text, like the promotions, the reviews, the night news debates—are far easier to glean than the text itself, which is an unsteady, slippery surface.

That his female protagonist is a Muslim not as much because he is so deeply moved by Muslim representation, or wants to resuscitate and mainstream their credo, as much as his imagination seems energized by the aesthetics of Islam—the turrets, the onion dome of a mosque, the *qaleen* weaving, the *mashallah*. This is not like the Manmohan Desai films of the '70s, '90s which forcefully included characters—however peripheral—from all religions to create this fictional tapestry that, hopefully, a secular country can feed off and recreate itself in the imprint of. If you see a character's religion foregrounded in a Bhansali film, they come with their specific, iconographic beauty. The Mona Lisa curtain in a Christian household; the arches of a Muslim household; the Holi of a Hindu household; the pleated frocks of the Christian household.

Even in songs, his Christian character Annie from *Khamoshi: The Musical* calls God 'khuda', not in some solidifying pan-religious gesture of faith, but because the way the word sits in the song, lyrics by Majrooh Sultanpuri, gives it that poetic lift he desires. His films have always foregrounded what things look like over what things are. For us to, then, brush past the appearance to revel in meaning—intended, imposed—feels like hitting a flat note.

To look at *Khamoshi: The Musical* and think it normalizes pre-marital sex, to watch *Guzaarish* and think that the film advocates euthanasia, to see in *Gangubai Kathiawadi* a film that is protesting at the picket fence screaming for the legalization of sex work, or to view *Heeramandi* as touched by the fervour of anti-colonialism, is to read these films thematically, meekly, too excited by their progressive prospects and socialist sheen. This approach forgets that even the director views politics as an excuse for celebration, not emancipation. He is chasing beauty, and *only* beauty. The story is an excuse. The image is the priority.

Submitting to his films, then, requires being a *sahridaya*—the person capable of experiencing *soundarya* or beauty, aligning yourself with the protagonist, being able to pulsate with that same grace, that same beauty. To be completely rapt. To be rendered incapable of rationality, drowned by a submissive, visceral creep.

Why am I bringing up the idea of soundarya, of sahridaya? What about these specific words eludes a perfect translation into English?

In aesthetic theory, a branch of philosophy which burned up in the eighteenth century with the German philosopher Alexander Gottlieb Baumgarten, there is a distinction made between an aesthetic experience and an aesthetic judgement. The former would be what the Portuguese poet Fernando Pessoa described as 'drifting without thoughts or emotions attending merely to my senses'.

Often what we fixate on is not the aesthetic experience but the aesthetic judgement—trying to condense what we feel into dispensable adjectives and puffy adverbs. This is how we now consume art, a consumption that is amenable to distillation.

However, professor of philosophy Bence Nanay in his book *Aesthetics: A Very Short Introduction* notes that the Indian 'Rasa Theory'—which goes back at least to Bharata's *Natyashastra* in the opening years of the Common Era, 2000 years ago—unlike the Western fixation of aesthetic judgement, is immersed in ideas of aesthetic experience, 'Judgments might work against the rasa.'[9]

The sahridaya, then, is a person whose impulse is towards aesthetic experience, not aesthetic judgement;

whose sensitivity allows what lecturer in Romanticism Shahidha Bari calls 'an unmistakable arrangement of attention and affect'[10]. As the late Professor B.N. Goswamy writes in his book *The Spirit of Indian Painting* 'The rasika—he who is sahridaya, meaning 'of the same heart'—must be competent, deserving, knowledgeable, who can bring utsaha to the act of viewing', utsaha being that pulsating joy. [11]

The twist is in what Goswamy says next, '[T]hat we can take from works of art only according to our own energies, or capacities', turning the tables of submission onto the spectator.

How to, then, be open to that 'ever-changing, flickering experience' in the theatre, one that Bhansali concocts with a pedantic, exaggerated affection? How to become a sahridaya as Bhansali's filmography streaks itself across one's life in the arts? And what do you have to renounce, leak out of you and leave behind, in order to step in?

I do concede that living in a fractured time has fractured our subjectivity. That we no longer see films as individuals, but we also see films keeping in mind some hypothetical spectator, some impressionable cub, wondering, what roulette is being pressed onto what mind. There is a strange, patronising attitude that has entered our spectatorship.

A while ago, on stage, somewhere in the heart of Dadar, I saw Odissi troupes bend their bodies with such lithesome grace, their very being broken into three by the *tribhanga*—bending at the knee, the hip, the neck—trying to create a lamp with their bodies, one dancer at the front, facing away from us, arms open wide and curved, like the clay lamp itself, and two dancers, like the flame on the wick, as though flickering in the wind, serpenting their bodies, their arms, and then, they move on, taking different shapes—as is wont in classical dance, the body becoming a vessel, malleable loam. This was part of a classical dance production, one of those events supported by the Ministry of Culture as part of their Azadi Ka Amrit Mahotsav campaign. Along with Odissi, there was Kathak and Bharatnatyam, the dancers and their gurus performing paeans to Bharat Mata, the flag waving, the musical Vande Mataram as a prayer-like refrain.

Every time these dancers turned their performance from the specifics of their narrative—like being a dove, like being a lamp—towards Bharat Mata, a sour taste curdled on my tongue, not just because in that moment the dancers seemed to abandon their sense of rhythm to do school-assembly flag-waving, but also because I was suddenly made aware that I was watching this performance at a moment when that very idea of Mother India feels betrayed, its social fabric in cosmic disarray. How could these artists, then, pretend this fracturing world does not exist?

How much of being a sahridaya, someone submitted, requires renouncing your links to your slowly eroding world?

This is a question people posed towards Bhansali in the aftermath of *Padmaavat*. Ziya Us Salam in his book *Being Muslim in Hindu India*, speaks of how this 'lopsided and biased projection of Alauddin Khilji is part of a larger project of the selective use of history to score points in our modern-day polity', of how the film—and its source text, written by a poet under Rajput patronage—refuses to even think of Khilji as someone beyond his evil slurpings.[12] The increasing demonization of the Muslim, of the Pakistani, as the genre of the patriotic action film took root, has been an ongoing problem in Hindi cinema.

Salam is right in claiming that *Padmaavat* is historically inaccurate, which even the film clarifies in its disclaimer, in its careful legal prose, noting that it is based on Malik Muhammad Jayasi's poem, 'which is considered a work of fiction'.

Salam quotes Katherine Schofield, a senior lecturer in South Asian music and history at King's College London, 'Film scholars talk about the historical film as providing a "heterotopia"—literally, "another place"—in which to play out the political and social issues of the present day. We should be reading these films not for what they tell us about the past . . . but what they tell us about us, now, in the present day.'

This reading, by insisting on the subtext, the context, is consciously keeping itself at a careful distance from the text itself—a common practice in criticism, because it is easier to grasp and growl at the subtext than luxuriate and thrash around in the text, especially when you are used to *thinking* through films as opposed to transcribing the experience of seeing it.

When Salam, taking the perspective of the 'masses' says, 'they cheered the Rajputs on loudly and jeered at the Sultanate king disdainfully, hatefully', he refuses to see how, in *Padmaavat*, the Rajput was actually a dull, frustrating icon of righteousness, while Khilji was delicious—sexually, ethically, narratively.

Evil has never been an excuse for Bhansali to dismiss characters, and this is part of the queerness with which he deals with them—the evil, gossipy aunt in *Hum Dil De Chuke Sanam*, the evil, envious sister-in-law in *Devdas*, the evil, monopolizing hijra politician in *Gangubai Kathiawadi*, the evil, scheming Brahmin priesthood in *Bajirao Mastani*, the evil huzoor of the *kotha* in *Heeramandi*, and her feuding partner. What is evil, he elevates to camp, and it is this campness that makes them more meaty, more exciting. To take a pejorative and twist it, fabulate it, celebrate it, such is the queerness of his filmography—there is almost something irresistible about them, and their wilful, exaggerated shirking of moral duties.

Then, to reduce characters to ideas, and pretending the 'masses'—which masses?—are responding to the ideas and not the characters, is one way of critiquing films like *Padmaavat*; where art is seen as a moral education, or one capable of providing a moral education or edification.

A more complicated—perhaps evasive, certainly nuanced—way would be to yoke the subtext to the text itself. Sometimes, this is more difficult, so full of suspicions we are, like me sitting in that auditorium, troubled, watching these dancers embody an idea as though it was untouched by the contemporary.

I ask myself, uncomfortably, if the dancers were more skilled, more supple in their artistry, would the soured politics of their performance have hiccupped for me? Do we only tighten our grip over the subtext and paratext when the text isn't compelling enough?

I want to float into this discussion the heady, heavily theorized, multiply-articulated concept of 'baroque'; I am drawing, specifically, on art critic Sebastian Smee who writes, 'Where Renaissance artists had treated the picture surface as a window onto scenes that kept the viewer at a chaste distance, Baroque artists burst this window open with sweeping dynamic arrangements, rich colour, and visceral brushwork.' To be able to, through seduction, 'transcend . . . programmatic dictates'[13]. Smee was thinking of the Baroque in the context of the painter Peter Paul Rubens, the sixteenth–seventeenth-century Flemish artist, and how it might be easy to read into his *Descent from the Cross* paintings, the counter reformation religious context which it was produced to service, but that would require experiencing the paintings at a barge-pole distance, because to press up against it would be to be seduced by the thickness of the brush strokes, the density and luminosity of colour, untroubled by the troubling context itself, not because the context does not exist, but because the consciousness is buried elsewhere, if only for a moment.

Sometimes, when all we grasp of art is its sublimated idea, something is lost in the act of spectatorship, even as another kind of radical clarity is gained. The trade-off, I suppose, of not being a sahridaya.

Perhaps, because of the blinkered blinding, beauty has garnered a terrible reputation as a fickle, superficial thing that, regardless, carries so much sociocultural significance. When science became the pinnacle of rationalism—science that can be experimented, observed, validated, contradicted, and slotted into categories of objective knowledge—beauty came to be seen as volatile, subjective, unstable, and thus unamenable to 'truth'. Truth came to be defined as an objective, verifiable claim, not an electric, seething pulse that escapes language, that exists outside of language. When people say 'beauty lies in the eyes of the beholder', they are essentially saying, what I see I cannot explain articulately enough to convince you, but I felt something, something that is true to me, and true to the time I experienced it in, and, perhaps, that truth cannot translate, that truth cannot exist outside of that moment I experienced it in.

What, then, is the point of beauty?

Well, perhaps, to argue that beauty has a point, that beauty must be stripped to its utility, its significance, is to miss the very point of beauty. When people look at Bhansali's films, rejecting it, what language are they using to express this rejection? That it is too much? That the story is too thin? That the staging isn't believable? All of this is a betrayal of beauty.

As Chloe Cooper Jones argues in her book *Easy Beauty*, leaning on philosopher Iris Murdoch, Beauty could help us improve the quality of our consciousness by briefly helping us "unself", gifting us a break from our "fat, relentless, ego", a reprieve from our expectations of what "good" and "bad" should be, from our hierarchies of art. To experience what Smee calls an 'animal immersion in the world'[14].

In some sense beauty is the opposite of knowledge. While knowledge makes us feel bigger, reaching out into the world, beauty makes the world feel bigger, towering over us. To write this book, attempting to forage a knowledge of beauty, is perhaps the ultimate irony, then, you can argue. How can anyone rationalize oneself into experiencing beauty, how can you cerebrally express the charms of the visceral? What I attempt here in this book, instead, is a desperation, trying to fling words at a feeling, hoping it will align with or approximate it, or at best, alleviate the doubts that crop up regarding these feelings, this beauty. My meditation on his filmography is both, trying to situate his cinema's beauty within a context of criticism by tapping into the visceral, and simultaneously, to fixate, cerebrally, on his films, hoping the cerebral might put some pressure on the visceral. There is something inherently strange and foolhardy about this, because what I am attempting to do is reorient your interiority, the way you lunge at the screen, and also my interiority, the way I lunge at the screen.

To focus on beauty, according to Jones, is to 'focus on the feeling of the world getting wider'. What Professor Priyadarshi Patnaik thinks of the creation of rasa, a 'nameless experience' that comes from a flood of 'forget[ting] our identities, our specific time and locale, our histories'[15].

To think of Bhansali's films, then—well, not to think, but to experience them—is to experience your smallness against the crashing tide of cinematic beauty. All we can do is submit, allow the self to glimmer into oblivion, if only for a snap. The least we could do is try.

Seeds Sown in *Khamoshi: The Musical*

To phir aao
Pyaar mein jalayein dil
Jalke bujh na paye dil

Come now
In love, let us burn
And burning, let us never extinguish

—Majrooh Sultanpuri

Set in seaside Goa, in a crumbling mansion with holes through which rainwater pitters and patters indoors, the sombre—and given Bhansali's later films, sober—*Khamoshi: The Musical* follows, episodically, the life of Annie (Manisha Koirala), the musically gifted daughter of poor, deaf, and mute parents—Joseph (Nana Patekar) and Flavia (Seema Biswas). As Annie grows into a woman, Raj (Salman Khan), a musician, wanders into her life, blindsiding her with charm and her future with possibility. They fall in love, and together chart a life as musicians who emerged from a world of silence, khamoshi.

Raj, the name, in Bhansali's world evokes the legacy of director-actor Raj Kapoor, whose peripatetic do-gooder characters of Nehruvian post-independent India were wandering, lonely, kind souls patching lives together, never imposing their interiority onto others.

Raj is not a character as much as a perfumed presence. He lives in lighthouses, writes in graveyards. Later, in *Saawariya*, too, Bhansali would name his male protagonist Raj—Ranbir Raj (played by Ranbir Kapoor, grandson of Raj Kapoor)—and there, too, he isn't bestowed with a background, with an origin, as though emerging out of ether. His is an unfussy, almost insubstantial Hinduism, willing to get married in a church with Annie, celebrate Christmas with her in *Khamoshi,* and Eid with Sakina in *Saawariya*. It is a name, a character that, like water, condenses into the shape provided by the woman he is in love with, and like water running through a sieve, leaving only its moistness behind. It is the kind of secular ideal that is achieved by effacing itself, becoming so pliable it diffuses.

Religious iconography is a way to substantiate character in Bhansali's films, and so when he refuses to root the religion of a character—like Raj the musician of *Khamoshi: The Musical* and *Saawariya*, like Sameer in *Hum Dil De Chuke Sanam*—he is also refusing to give them context. They become airy ideals that float around giving the film its fragrance, but never its foundation.

Khamoshi: The Musical begins in the present. Raj and Annie are married with a kid, on their way to visit Joseph and Flavia. 'Huyya Huyya', the energetic kitsch song, introduces the four of them. The words 'Huyya Huyya' mean nothing, like the introductory babble of 'Aaj Mein Upar', like 'Tattad Tattad' in *Ram-Leela*. Meaning has been subsumed to feeling. Bhansali, with his lyricist Majrooh Sultanpuri is asking: when you hear these words, these sounds given phonetic shape, what are you feeling—not thinking, but feeling?

Joy, yes?

We have entered the world of Bhansali, where men make an entrance perched on a car brimming with flowers, women drape a table with cloth that flutters as they dust it into place, where gowns cinched at the waist float in the air as women twirl—chiffon, cotton. These are not your regular gowns, despite draping poor bodies; their poverty is textual, not visual, and often this sandpapering friction between the textual and the visual can be disorienting, because poverty is used as a narrative convenience to push a story along, with the film itself refusing to buy into the consequences of its aesthetic choices. Costumes Designed by Manish Malhotra, there is lace on the neck, on the cuffs, with netted headdresses and loose fabrics tied around the neck that adds a visual dynamism to small things like a walk or a run or a circumambulation. Grace is mundane.

This cinematic poverty, however un-poverty-like, came in 1996, when Hindi cinema was being swept up by another, counter obsession, in the haze of the 1991 liberalization of the economy, with the diaspora-facing glint in the eyes of the filmmakers, and protagonists with leather jackets and branded tight shirts and dresses. As author Arundhati

Roy says, 'Pre-the 1990s, pre-corporate, neoliberal globalization, you see in Bollywood a great respect for the poor . . . The heroes of Bollywood, they were trade union leaders, they were people who came out of the slums, they were workers in mills and so on. From the 1990s, the poor began to be erased from culture, from cinema,' being replaced by 'a new imagination, the imagination of unlimited greed, of capitalism, of boastful wealth and those thousand-seater cinemas were all disappearing and the cinema halls became these plush multiplexes with very expensive tickets. Poor people don't go to those places and cinema came to be confected for this new audience.'[1]

Roy is looking at the disappearance of the poor protagonist alongside the shuttering of single screens, almost as twin forces. The single screen theatres could only show one movie at a time—big theatres, often in colonial buildings, uncomfortable seats, cheap tickets—while the new multiplex cinema, with leather seats that recline, could simultaneously show many movies in smaller auditoriums. They were often lodged in malls which, despite having free entry, doused certain kinds of bodies with certain kinds of suspicions—as though they do not belong there.

There was another facet to this transition—the falling apart of single screen theatres. Director Vishal Bhardwaj watched the 'first day first show' of his debut film *Makdee* (2002) in a single screen theatre. He told journalist Uday Bhatia, '*Uss samay theatres ka bahut bura haal tha*' (Theatres were in bad shape in those days) . . . I was seeing the screen through the fan.' For his next film, the breakout *Maqbool*, the premiere was organized in a multiplex cinema. 'The face of the cinema changed because of the multiplexes . . . People had stopped going to the cinema because there were rats in the theatres and the air-conditioning and quality of the seats was appallingly bad. So, people used to watch in their homes on pirated CDs. But when multiplexes came, that audience started coming to the theatres,' Bhardwaj told Bhatia.[2]

It was PVR that pioneered the multiplex revolution in India, establishing the first multiplex cinema in 1997 at Saket, New Delhi. Today, across 359 locations, the recently merged PVR INOX has 1712 screens. When you go to watch a movie in these theatres, in Mumbai at least, you are told to stand for the national anthem by a voice in an American accent.

The single screens, on the other hand, have plummeted—from around 24,000 single screens in 1990, there were barely 6000 still functioning in 2022,[3] with most of them clustered in the South, where cinematic macho heroism is still animated by poverty.

What was happening here was not just pandering to a different kind of audience, but also a shift in the very idea of a fantasy, which columnist Damien Walter defined as 'the total eradication of self . . . fuelling our ravenous appetite for escape'[4].

The best fantasies feel real, producing this dual, contradictory pressure. One the one hand, it helps 'unself' the self, producing immersion in a world and time elsewhere, and on the other, it furiously 'selves' you, making you aware of your body, your thoughts, your aspirations, tapping into it with a depth of feeling even as it peddles in alternate realities, laws, possibilities, flirting with the absurd, and sometimes, becoming it.

This tension—between what is real, what is glazed—is best expressed in the cinema of Karan Johar, which emerged in the mid-1990s, full of candied stories of love and characters whose lives you want to, simultaneously, escape into, and aspirationally inhabit one day, some day. It is this vigorous self-ing and unself-ing that makes his cinema this robust site of desire. You lean into it just enough, seeing faint threads of your present self and future-aspired self floating around the narrative somewhere; punctures of mimesis.

Take the costume design of Johar's first film *Kuch Kuch Hota Hai*. The main protagonist Rahul, in college, was dressed in Polo Sports and DKNY—brands that were out of reach of most people in the newly globalized India. Out of reach, but the reach was still visible, possible, even if implausible. It didn't feel like an intergalactic, impossible desire. So, while, on the one hand, Karan Johar was spinning the most egregious tale of love lost and returned, of shunning realism so effectively that to ask for it would render you inane, on the other hand, when it came to his costumes, he did not merely want it to *signal* richness—he wanted it to *be* rich. You can doubt the veracity of anything on-screen, never the richness of the protagonist; a richness that has leaked from Johar's life itself, the actors borrowing clothes from his wardrobe. Suddenly, with this possibility of this narrow realism, the larger fantasy became juicier.

This shifted your relationship with the film. You were alert to not just the story unfolding, but also to its branded, aesthetic gloss. Manish Malhotra, who began his career as a costume designer for films like *Kuch Kuch Hota Hai*, launched his own couture label in 2005, connecting that thread of aspiration from the film to his store. His name is now synonymous with weddings—both on and off-screen. Karan Johar's films—the ones he makes, the ones he produces—are now a site of both aesthetic and narrative aspiration. I graduated from high school around *Yeh Jawani Hai Deewani's* (2014) release, and I remember the palpable tension the cobalt blue Manish Malhotra sari with a sequinned border and a ruffled gold trimming Deepika Padukone wore in 'Badtameez Dil' caused, wondering who would wear it to the farewell ceremony? (The prettiest in the batch, it was assumed). The sari was rendered iconic by repetition. Vogue India did a piece on how you can recreate the look. This was not a mimetic desire to be Deepika Padukone's character but to look like her—a distinction that cinematic fantasies make and melt, replacing appearance for essence.

In this context, *Khamoshi* and Bhansali's cinema, generally, was a bit of a countercultural force, even as it sputtered away at the box office. A countercultural force, perhaps, just in theory. It did not encourage mimesis. It resisted globalization. It thoroughly rejected reality. It refused to *want* to leak into your life, content being fluttered on the screen, *out there*. The only bridge it wanted to make between the screen and you was not of aspiration, but beauty.

There is an uninterrupted thirty-second shot in 'Huyya Huyya' of Flavia dancing inside a thatch shed with sharp afternoon light flooding from all directions, creating a cross-hatched patch of light over her as the camera, in a dizzy, drunken trail, rotates around her. Salman Khan, joyous, energetic, thrusts his hips with Koli women. It is not just beautiful, it is playful, too, and a little silly. Bhansali's craft, even while excessive and gilded, has cracks from which emerge the most garish humour. A fart in *Hum Dil De Chuke Sanam* or pornographic jokes in *Ram-Leela*. It is only when he moves into history—*Bajirao Mastani, Padmaavat*—that humour is dulled out of the narrative, replaced by a regal posturing that coats his cinematic world.

As the joy of 'Huyya Huyya' subsides, Raj and Annie are shrapnelled in a car accident. Annie is in a coma, but her voice guides us into a flashback of her life. The flashback device anchoring the film is used sparingly in Bhansali's filmography—only in films with female protagonists leading us into their storied past, in *Black,* in *Saawariya*, and in *Gangubai Kathiawadi*; the flashback, the desire to look behind you and narrate your past, make sense of it, cohere it, as feminine. Almost a gesture inviting the spectator to bear witness to their life. Here, see my world.

Bhansali's men rarely find the need to look back at their life, usually thrusting forward into a bedlam of their own making. Why should men remember? (In *Guzaarish*, it is a bedridden Ethan Mascarenhas, who, every now and then, looks back with regret and longing at his life as a magician, the only example of a Bhansali hero bending back into time, dipping into memories with fragmented pain, not coherent confidence, without a voice-over, unlike his women.)

In *Khamoshi: The Musical*, we can see brewing a narrative trend that Bhansali will keep returning to over the course of his career. One is the penchant to turn everything, even grief, into song, into celebration. When the family, in a dire financial strait, has to sell the piano, Annie's grandmother, Mariamma (Helen) begins a dance with the men who are ferrying the piano away. A moment of separation has been recast as one of bittersweet farewell, '*Gaate the pehle akele, aaj gaata hai saara jaahan*', that the piano and its music was once ours, and now as we say farewell, it belongs to the world. Helen's face is placed between that of the kids who are seated on the piano, their back to us, on either side of the frame, as the piano is lugged across the beach. The piano rotates, the kids sitting on it are rotating too, and the light on Helen's face moves from being fully lit to being half dunked in shadows, teaching the kids the lesson of loss inflected by one of hope.

Bhansali revels in this *khatta-meetha* (sweet and sour) texture of life, where even joy is tinted with melancholy and grief with fortitude. The use of something humorous, a game, a joke, like twisting the ear to cause the tongue to purr out, is later used when Annie is in a coma. On something playful has been poured pathos. Even later, in *Hum Dil De Chuke Sanam*, the 'statue' game, rib-tickling and silly, is later used when the lovers part, him stunning her, 'statue', so she cannot move, but is frozen in longing as he departs.

In interviews, Bhansali loves expressing, explaining the inflections of pain in his art as biographical scratches that he lends his characters—a child growing up in the Bhuleshwar chawls in Mumbai, next to the red-light district of Kamathipura. The scene of Annie going door-to-door selling soap can be traced to Bhansali's childhood, when he and his sister accompanied their mother as she sold wares from home to home. The scene where the record is broken, too, was a cinematic sublimation of his father, in frustration, breaking his records. Even his recurring fixation with the Christian and Anglo-Indian community, which he will pull at in *Black*, and later, *Guzaarish*, he attributes to his teachers, observing their eating habits and the red wine served in crystal glasses in their homes.

What began with *Khamoshi: The Musical* was not just Bhansali's career but him edifying his legacy on celluloid by staging his piecemeal biographies. He was orchestrating his myth *through* his movies, which were acquiring a mythical status of their own.

This also throws light on Bhansali's inability to stew in joy in his films. He won't ever pile joy with more joy, while he has no issues sedimenting sadness with more sadness, and then, some more sadness. A carefully plotted narrative zigzagging through emotions, joy only comes in brief, bright pockets. So, the flashback becomes this alternating patchwork of thin euphoria and loaded melancholy. When Mariamma dies, that emptiness allows for Willie (Raghuvir Yadav), their neighbour to saunter in, introducing Annie to the world of recorded music. Later, when Annie and Raj promise each other to work hard and build a career, a life in music, beyond Goa, it is immediately followed by Flavia's heart attack, which further drives Annie's need to be at home. A promise of freedom, of hope, scraped at by a vow of subservience—to always be with her parents, to be *their* voice.

There is something neat about this structure, and with this neatness comes a suspicion, because every emotion begins to feel like an excuse for it to be upturned. The language of the film lays itself bare.

Khamoshi: The Musical is Bhansali's most emotionally pure film. Purity not as a virtue but as an uncluttered state of cinema. His ideas of beauty—the grand stain on his stories—were germinating here, but never fully expressed with the scale and audacity he would later wield confidently. So, submitting to this film is an act of submitting to its emotional landscape, not its exaggerated staging. You are moved by the characters and their grief, not the awe that spins their pathos skywards. There is never a doubt about where to locate your visceral lunge towards this film.

Both Flavia and Joseph cannot grasp melody because they are deaf, but they can still *feel* rhythm. When Flavia presses her ear against a young Annie's chest as she sings, trying to feel the varying shapes of her breath, or when Mariamma, gets Joseph's attention while he is hammering the roof into place, telling him to instead hammer to the rhythm of the song Annie is playing on the piano by showing him the spaces between the notes—these are moments dense with love and loss, longing and joy.

These, to Jatin–Lalit's melody, still tug at something soft. When Joseph screams looking at his young son, Annie's brother, who fell from the church roof to his death, it is a primal howl; you are pummelled. Compared to this, note how grief is expressed in his later films—as ballistic, balletic, always stylized, elevating the scene beyond the story.

It becomes clear that *Khamoshi: The Musical* is not, essentially, Raj and Annie's love story. Nor is it about Annie's musical career, for neither are complicated nor challenged in the movie. Their love and her career soar. These narrative deferrals—of their love, of her voice finding its way beyond the coast—come without much fuss. What is the 'story', then?

This, often, is a jerk for people watching Bhansali's cinema—the expectation of a simple story that can be condensed into an articulate line. Bhansali thwarts such expectations. With *Saawariya* and *Guzaarish*, he spun around a wafer-thin plot; you marvelled at the reckless confidence. With *Devdas* and *Ram-Leela*, he threaded an epic in such monstrously odd directions, you marvelled at the subversion, not just in the writing but in the casting, too.

He takes Hrithik Roshan, known for his physical beauty, his ripped, marble-like body, and makes him, in *Guzaarish*, a paraplegic with a ballooning stomach, showing us how he needs help even brushing his teeth, parting his dry lips in the morning. Even when he cast Aishwarya Rai Bachchan as the Gujarati belle with a serpentine plait in *Hum Dil De Chuke Sanam*, or when he cast Shah Rukh Khan to play the alcoholic, lovelorn Devdas, a role that Dilip Kumar immortalized, there was a hissing, palpable doubt. Bhansali was clear, 'He has beautiful eyes.' With his last film *Gangubai Kathiawadi*, there was an almost unanimous anxiety about how Alia Bhatt's face, untouched by adulthood, attached as it was to headstrong, pouty youthisms in *2 States* (2014) and *Dear Zindagi* (2016) and peppy romantic comedies where sex feels like a sweet plaything in the *Dulhaniya* films, could conjure the violation and volition of the brothel madam. It was a leap that not only her as an artist, but we too, as spectators, had to make—to reimagine the face in contexts we would never have imagined it in, arguing its malleability.

This question becomes more urgent with *Gangubai Kathiawadi* because calling something 'innocent' is invariably to repress its sexuality, as the scholar in psychoanalysis Jacqueline Rose noted in her analysis of the forever child of literature, Peter Pan. With that in mind, how can an innocent face, then, inhere the interiority of dirty, violative sex?

Yet, that is the contradiction that forms the bedrock of Bhatt's sharply observed performance, where she weaponized this innocence to create a character who wears that contradiction on her sleeve. At no point are we allowed to forget the innocence that was erased and written over to produce a 'madam', a politician, a protector. When she puts her hands on the back of a bench, seated cross-legged, looking out into the world; when she sits next to her lover whom she's married off to another, sunglasses on, ankles of one leg on the knee of the other, a spread out posture; when she puts her feet on the chair in front of her, flipping a beedi onto her lips; when she walks putting the pressure of all her weight on each step—every gesture is a forceful act of un-making that innocence. It doesn't come naturally, and yet, it doesn't feel uncomfortable, uncharacteristic. To not forget that she is the boss, and to not forget that she was wrenched out of her childlike idyll to become this boss. In this performance, as in many others, it is adulthood that has to be performed clinically and strategically, as though innocence is what comes naturally and anything else involves an effort.

In an interview, she invoked this very innocence, that very criticism thrown at her: '[Gangubai's] innocence and her vulnerability was intact, despite having to play this very strong role for these women.' When Bhansali was building parallels with her performance, he invoked Nargis from *Mother India* (1957), Seema Biswas from *Bandit Queen* (1994), Meena Kumari in *Saheb Biwi Aur Ghulam* (1962); that Bhatt's Gangubai stands alongside these performances, in his hall of fame, all women of deep, grunting pathos, but also stands apart. Her performance does not lean into the connotations of her face, but rubs up against it; that while Kumari, Nargis, and Biswas had a bracing gravity to their gaze that lent itself to their performance of tragedy, Bhatt's pathos comes from a face, a gaze, where youth still lives. If not desecrated, many of these anxieties diminished with the release of the films.

Similarly, Bhansali takes Nana Patekar and Seema Biswas, known for their sharp, charismatic dialogue delivery, with Biswas coming out of the raves of *Bandit Queen*, and makes them mute in *Khamoshi*. Also, strangely, Manisha Koirala, who was, at the time, having an alleged affair with Patekar, plays his daughter in this film. There is a deep irreverence here, a slipperiness, almost like he is trying to evade not just the expectations of the time, but your grasp as a viewer, as a fan, as a critic.

How, then, to speak of *Khamoshi*?

Khamoshi is, instead, about Annie's journey through life, and how, in one of these chapters, Raj enters, and she finds and pursues music, even as her heart is torn between her future and her parents. This dichotomy—one's future, one's parents—will keep coming up through his films, exerting opposing forces in the lives of his protagonists. The emotional violence, then, stems from this opposition—that a protagonist needs to transcend the demands of their parents even as they are limited by it.

As we flip forward through Bhansali's filmography, however, this opposition ceases to put pressure on the narrative as parents leak out, their opinions, their antagonism (*Ram-Leela*, *Bajirao Mastani*), or even their meekly sketched presence (*Saawariya, Guzaarish*, *Padmaavat, Gangubai Kathiawadi*) having little to no discernible impress on their lives. The vice-like grip of parental opposition to personal love is, instead, in films like

Saawariya and *Guzaarish* replaced with a more internal circadian, anguished rhythm, and in his later films, post *Ram-Leela*, with a grand societal spectacle of a battle, his characters battling not mothers and fathers, but people, crowds and identities.

It is impossible to describe any of Bhansali's films—which all hinge on an obsessive, pungent love—as love stories, because he is so unworried about their destiny, so indifferent to what happens in the 'end'. The idea of love-stories using 'barriers' and 'conflicts' to defer the eventual consummation is flung out of the window. Deferral is an eternal state in his movies. That lovers must love forever seems bizarre to Bhansali. That they met, that they loved, however briefly, is more tantalizing to him. He is more excited by what separation, what death, what sacrifice does to that love. Does it still remain? Does it still throb?

In an interview with Karan Thapar, Bhansali noted, 'It is not important to be loved. It is important to love.' When Thapar interjected, 'But unrequited love . . . ', Bhansali snapped back, 'It is painful, so what?'[5]

But despite not being, primarily, about love, *Khamoshi* introduces what Bhansali considers his grand theory of love, when a priest advises Raj, '*Pyaar besabri nahin, pyaar sirf khushi nahin, pyaar gunah bhi nahin, dukh bhi, sabr bhi, intezaar bhi.*' Love isn't impatience, love isn't only happiness, love isn't sin, it is sadness, too, patience, too, longing, too. To fall in love in Bhansali's films is to invite chaos into your life, to suffuse it with sweet longing and acrid anxiety. Often, to love is to be heartbroken. *Khamoshi* is the only Bhansali film where a lover isn't left lurking, alone or grieving in the end. In all his subsequent films, either the lover is left out of a triangle, the lover dies, or the lover sacrifices their love. A reflection of Guru Dutt's filmography, which also began with joy and lovers meeting (*Mr and Mrs 55*), but soon developed into a writhing compendium of heartbreak and loneliness (*Pyaasa*, *Kaagaz Ke Phool*).

The lover is, to Bhansali, god. When Raj looks at Annie, puts his hands out and sings, 'Tell me O Khuda'; when Sakina in *Saawariya* prays to Ranbir Raj, folding her hands over his, and sings, '*Haan magar yeh sach hai, mere bhagwan ho tum*', that it is true, you are my god; when Paro touches Devdas' feet after getting married to someone else. There is a spiritual reading of this that I do not find insightful or moving. In fact, it is rather trite.

What, instead, I am excited by is how, by making the lover god, by making the act of love one of submission, Bhansali is able to bring in sex without showing it. Sex, too, is an act of submission, away from the gaze of what is permissible or respectable. It allows you to discover your limits, or the fact that you have none. It allows you to dissolve your dignity. It allows pleasure in pain. It insists on pain in pleasure. This is how Bhansali conceives of love, too, on your knees, looking up.

Khamoshi: The Musical is Bhansali's most religious film, where one of the main arcs the narrative stews in is that of Joseph rejecting Christ, throwing the cross into the sea after the death of his son, to ultimately, in the end, embrace that very cross. The film ends with the inane line, 'He can hear us. God is never silent.' It is in his later films that he would invoke religion as, merely but substantially, an aesthetic choice.

There is nothing spiritual about these gods that give the character comfort, there is no quest for cosmic meaning.

It gives him excuses for celebration, for showcasing the inherent spectacle of the festivals. Religion also gives Bhansali a reason for his characters, his female characters, to be coy, graceful. When he wants to give them erotic fire—like he did with Leela in *Ram-Leela*, like Gangubai in *Gangubai Kathiawadi*—he makes them godless, their irreverence expressed as atheism or agnosticism or at least a cultural distance from faith, even as they ripple outwards in their garba. Think of the sex workers he has depicted in his cinema—Chandramukhi's graceful faith in *Devdas*, steeped in becoming a Mira-like devotee of Devdas, going to temples, lighting lamps, contrasted with Gulab's erotic fire in *Saawariya,* where she sings an old film song while 'praying'. To be erotic is to be faithless, because to be erotic is to be self-sufficient, without any need for spiritual or emotional succour from some higher power, because to be erotic is already to be submitted.

~

Khamoshi: The Musical introduces two important aesthetic choices that Bhansali would follow throughout his career that we discussed in the introduction. One was the long shot. The other is the top shot.

The long shot, as a cinematic choice, is the closest we get from seeing cinema as aligned to reality, because every second spent on-screen, during a scene, becomes a second spent by you as a spectator. It is a perfect alignment with time's forward thrust. There is no fast forwarding through a story, no edit choice that tinkers with a scene, tightening it, trucking through it. I am fascinated by how this long shot allows the rhythm of cinema to condense upon the rhythm of life itself, till they ebb and flow as one.

When Raj and Annie first tell each other they are in love with one another, when Raj later confronts Annie after she repeatedly ghosts him—all of these are long shots, with Annie and Raj facing each other, their side profiles being served to us in an extended moment of yearning.

When you think of what the single long shot does, think of the alternatives it forsakes. An over-the-shoulder shot where we get complete access to the actors' faces? A wide shot where you see how this couple is alone, on the balcony of the top floor of a house by the shore at night, or at the top of a lighthouse during a hazy afternoon? This is Bhansali taking your attention, shoving it towards his character, and telling you, 'This, right here, is more beautiful than anything else.' Bhansali's beauty, as you can see, isn't always the most obvious choice.

To think that from the, literally, infinite number of angles from which a scene could be shot, that could run for an infinite number of lengths, we get to see just *one* of those many possibilities.

When Raj runs behind Joseph across a beach trying to convince him that he will be a suitable groom for Annie, Bhansali decides to have it as a long shot, trailing with the runners, as though the scene is touched by the cadence of life. This allows you to see the emotional negotiation that takes place on the face of Joseph, the way Raj is trying to navigate the vicissitudes of it, his amenability to Raj's charm, but his deep suspicion of it. It is why he holds the camera as characters erupt, using the cinematic language of a long shot to impress upon us the unedited fragment of their lives. Take the scene where Annie is thrown out of the house by her father after she announces she is pregnant, and she shrieks her resentments at the slatted door. This preference for long shots allows for life and beauty in the cracks of it to transpire. It also lays bare the limitations of the actors. That Salman Khan cannot hold onto the intensity of a moment is clear from the multiple scenes where he is expected to do just that. That Manisha Koirala only bursts into animation, to then retreat, is clear. The chinks of the acting armoury suddenly emerge to the surface.

In his songs, too, Bhansali allows the shot to linger for as long as possible, so we can see the gestures, the movements emerge from the body till the final pose. When Annie is singing by the mic, you see her hands—interpreting the song for her parents—move from the heart to point to them. It isn't interrupted by giving us another angle, another emphasis. Seen another way, this is Bhansali's deep reverence towards dance, towards the choreographer, towards the character, and his irreverence towards us, the attention-split audience. We should keep pace with him, not the other way round.

Bhansali's fixation with top shots—a perfectly symmetrical viewfinder as fabrics flare or myriad banana leaves turn open in a simultaneous rustle beneath, like in *Bajirao Mastani*—is part of his visible craft. In *Khamoshi: The Musical* you can see hints of this style emerging, with his camera trying to go as high as possible to look down, but Bhansali's world hadn't yet evolved into the high ceiling palaces yet, and neither was the technology accessible enough to place a camera in the skies, looking down. This would burst open with *Hum Dil De Chuke Sanam*—during the songs.

In interviews, he refers to the top shot, rather pretentiously, as the view of god. But the top shot is a fascinating point of view, to look at an event from above, an access humans are usually never allowed. If the long shot allows the distance between the protagonist and the spectator to diminish into dust, the top shot allows the spectator to see what they have been evolutionarily denied, what the protagonist can never see, to replace physical presence with cinematic presence. It is, perhaps, in some sense, godly. It is also, in the age of drone photography, where top shots are often mistaken for world-building, a purely aesthetic puncture, a rip of perspective.

Khamoshi: The Musical released on 9 August 1996, and despite having Salman Khan who had tasted fame with *Andaz Apna Apna* (1994), *Hum Aapke Hain Koun..!* (1994) and *Karan Arjun* (1995), and Manisha Koirala fresh out *1942: A Love Story* (1994) and *Bombay* (1995), the film flopped on arrival. On the Friday of its release, Bhansali got an early morning call from his producer who ominously noted, 'Picture baith gayi'. This was the first time Bhansali had heard this phrase, trade-speak for a film tanking. The film wasn't even given a chance to compete.

Cinematographer Anil Mehta remembers, 'I was told you've shot the film in black and white, and I think Sanjay was told you have made a documentary.' No one seemed to have got the film, its pace too slow, its focus too watery.

The set designer Nitin Chandrakant Desai, the editor Bela Segal, and Bhansali went from theatre to theatre, looking at the reaction, and cutting the film down on the spot. But the ship had sunk, and nothing could yank it out of the trenches. Hurt but not without hope, Bhansali's canvas only became wider, more riotous, more ambitious, and many would argue, more indulgent. His successes would be dizzying, and his failures would be like a vertiginous plunge, both spoken about for weeks after the release, mythologized, much like his life story. Every film's birthing felt ominous, as though it was an inflection point, a crowning high or the plonking gravestone on his career—one entrenched in pursuit of beauty.

He boomeranged back, though, three years later, with *Hum Dil De Chuke Sanam*, what Mehta believes was his film 'on the rebound'[6].

The vengeance could be seen in the contrast. The poor Goan-Christian household was swapped for an upper class, upper caste monument, the Vijaya Vilas Palace. The deaf and mute household glissando-ed into a steeply musical family. White has been dyed over, *bandhani* blooming in blouses, the pleated frocks are now starched, flaring lehengas in metallic colours, Manish Malhotra is now Neeta Lulla. As though Bhansali was twisting his style into a tighter, more discernible key.

What remains the same is love which comes out of nowhere—Salman Khan again, as Sameer, who has come from Italy to learn music from Pandit Darbar (Vikram Gokhale)—perfuming the life of Nandini (Aishwarya Rai Bachchan), daughter of Pandit Darbar. They pursue this courtship under the nose of the extended family and yet are never caught.

Eight months later, they *are* caught, and it is only *then* we are told that eight months have passed. In between there was a Diwali celebration—which rolls the film into being—a marriage, and Makar Sankranti; celebration as an excuse to put forward Bhansali's preference for eruption of beauty through which the film's emotional postures are clarified, its timeline clicked into alignment, the world tied to a calendar.

Everything feels condensed. If you told me this was a month's worth of courtship, I would have believed it. That this affair feels timeless is to say that this affair does not require time to make sense, that it is untouched by the forward motion, the linear sedimenting of love. He does something similar in a film like *Bajirao Mastani*, where love moves from a glance to an expression, to marriage, to childbirth, to death. There is no sense of space and time between these moments; they exist outside the scene. Like starburst, the love immediately, rapturously, consummately corrodes the surface of their lives.

And much like time doesn't really glide from one moment to the next, space, too, in his movies, leapfrogs. Space is fragmented even as we are often given wide shots, top shots to present space as unified. You will never know which rooms lead to where, unless your heroine runs through the space as in *Hum Dil De Chuke Sanam* and *Devdas* or walks through it as in *Black* and *Guzaarish*. In *Hum Dil De Chuke Sanam*, the locations swarm between Kutch, Bhuj, Rann, and Jaisalmer, all woven into one place. Later, Hungary will be shown as Italy, as though the difference between the two, an allegiance to realism, is of no importance. Bhansali, a fan of Hungarian filmmakers István Szabó and István Gaál, whom he got acquainted with at FTII, insists that he wanted to shoot the film there as an homage, but since Budapest did not have a ready recall among Indian audiences, he chose to call it Italy. (It is also much cheaper to shoot in Hungary than Italy.)

So pungent are these frames that establish their love, that the leaps of time and fractures of space feel irrelevant. Bhansali is, after all, chasing moments. He isn't interested in how they tie up into the space-time fabric. This is, perhaps, what many mean when they call his films timeless, suspended. It is not a criticism or a praise as much as a characterization of his worlds. Though, it also sours as a limitation, that Bhansali is unable to stay with a character and see them through, obsessed as he is with fixated moments—cinematically, through the long shots, narratively, through the dense attention given to this discrete moment. What emerges can feel incomplete, like shards that we consume as a smooth surface.

When Nandini and Sameer's simmering love is caught, he is told to leave, his departure to Italy being his *guru dakshina*. Nandini is carted off in marriage to young lawyer Vanraj (Ajay Devgn), a more suitable boy. Vanraj soon finds out about the affair, but in a twist of both sympathy and saviour complex, he decides to go to Italy—Hungary, really—with Nandini to find Sameer and reunite them.

It is here we see an early articulation of idealized masculinity in Bhansali's cinema. Vanraj is asked by his father how he can take his wife all the way to Italy so she can reunite with her lover, '*Kahan gayi tumhari mardaangi?*', where has your masculinity gone?

Vanraj replies, '*Kya mardaangi aurat ko kamzor maankar, uski khushiyon par zabardasti qaboo karne mein hai? Kya mardaangi sacchai se munh chupane ka doosra naam hai? Kya mardaangi us aurat ke saath rehna hai jiska jism toh aapka ho lekin uska dil, uski aatma kisi aur ki hai? . . . Mardaangi haqeeqat aur mushkilon ka saamna karne mein hai.*'

Is masculinity that which makes men consider women weak, imposing our will on them, shackling them? Is masculinity that which conceals the truth? Is masculinity that which gives access to her body, but never her soul, which throbs for elsewhere? . . . Masculinity is that which confronts reality and the problems it throws up.

That Vanraj, an anomaly in Bansali's filmography for reasons I will get into shortly, is the one professing this theory of masculinity, touched by pathos and poetry, is fascinating. Perhaps, it is because he is a lawyer. This is a strange profession to have in this world. Bhansali's heroes are artists—musicians, singers, magicians—or loafers. They do not have a sense of their economic value to society, nor do they crave it. In the post-liberalization world in which films like *Khamoshi* and *Hum Dil De Chuke Sanam* are made and consumed, these male figures cut an odd figure, because the films surrounding it are full of idealized bodies being carted off in coats and suits, aware of and tending to their utility to the economy, to the family. It is, often, the women who work—as singers, caretakers, courtesans, carpet weavers—but their working is never allowed to demean the masculinity of their lost, male counterparts, as it would in conventional narratives. Think of how, in *Aashiqui* (1990), in *Abhimaan* (1973), when both lovers are artists, the woman's success is seen at the cost of the man's, but in *Khamoshi*, one helps build the other.

Bhansali's men are unblemished by neoliberal anxieties of utility. And when he finds the one white collar job for one of his characters—a lawyer—he makes him a paragon of sacrifice, giving up his life, his marriage, and in the eyes of his father, his masculinity. These are not offsprings of that terrible being, Homo Economicus.

The surface of *Hum Dil De Chuke Sanam*, also scrubbed and framed by Anil Mehta, is an extension of *Khamoshi*, with both still and frenetic shots, long shots and close-ups, and no glaring visual preference. Though more grand, more colourful, it was coming out of and replicating something familiar, just exploded in scale, a rainbow riot let loose. It is also psychologically more astute. When Sameer is made to sing in front of Pandit Darbar for the first time to prove his *gayaki*, he rips out into a Western funk to the Pandit's disappointment, and the camera moves in closer when the beat starts its percussive purr, only for him to swerve into classical—who else but Shankar Mahadevan to vocalize this swerve—and the camera with its vertical jerk almost lugs close to Mahadevan's vocals that have hit a high note and stay there, with breath as a mere formality. Here is the camera aiding, adding to the emotional text.

Later, during a fierce altercation between families, the camera unhinges itself from the stationary position and snakes, hand-held, into their faces, expressing the splintering, sputtering energy of the scene.

In one of the most stunning displays of acting being enhanced by direction and the uncircumcised shot, we have Nandini's father, framed in side profile, looking anxious. His daughter has just attempted suicide. Her potential in-laws are at the door. The camera stays still, and he does a 180-degree turn, and the anxiety melts into a smile one performs for the guest.

Later, in Italy, when Vanraj and Nandini mistake a jestering, comical Indian for Sameer, this patient framing trembles the surface of the scene. Vanraj and Nandini are sitting side by side on a moving tram. Vanraj is smiling, entertained by how weird the 'wrong' Sameer was. Nandini is hurt. She looks at him, and her hurt morphs into annoyance, then deep despair as a teardrop, like pearls being spun, forms and quickly descends for her to wipe it off. Vanraj looks at her, and his smile traipses into concern.

All of this is to point out that while the auteur theory holds—the idea that a director is the central writer of a film, metabolizing the various strands into a unified voice that gets honed through repetition—the labour of that artistry is being spread out, the voice of the director emerging from the symphony, not as *one* voice, but a chorus. As we snake through Bhansali's filmography, we cannot forget the artists he collaborated with in the various stages of his fermenting, for they have lent themselves to his auteurship, twisting it, adding to it, editing it with their artistry, the auteur not as a singular, but a steered, collective voice.

Darshan in *Devdas*

Sheeshe se sheesha takraye, jo bhi ho anjaam
Oh dekho kaise
chalaka chalaka chal
chalaka chalaka chal
chalaka chalaka chalkaye re

As glass collides with glass, no sense of consequence
Oh, look how the glass spills
chalaka chalaka chal

—Nusrat Badr

Sure, the film is named after its male protagonist, but the entry scene—that sacred moment of commercial cinema where a star scratches, like a cat against a carpet, his presence on celluloid as a character, neither renouncing stardom, nor embracing an effacing artistry—is reserved for the female protagonist. Really, one of two female protagonists. Really, one of three entry scenes.

Paro, or Parvati, (Aishwarya Rai Bachchan) is introduced lamp-first, her hands—with fingers capped with *alta*—holding it gently. For ten years she has been waiting for her childhood love, Devdas (Shah Rukh Khan), to return from London. In his absence, she sublimated her erotic attention towards this lamp—one whose wick she kept oil-licked and flame-tended for all these ten years in the hope that this dedicated, disciplined devotion will make Devdas curl back home, to Bengal.

Though, of course, the Bengali-ness of this world, like the Gujarati-ness of *Hum Dil De Chuke Sanam* and, later, *Ram-Leela*, and the Marathi-ness of *Bajirao Mastani*, is expressed as an exaggeration, the accents overwrought in places, watery in some, forgotten in others, fermenting elsewhere, and this is because identity, for Bhansali, is a performance, not a thing you breathe with, and performances are, infamously, shaky and fragile. Besides, Bhansali is not working with characters as much as apparitions; these vaporized beings—it is impossible to find in them an empathetic depth to cling to, to find yourself in them, to relate to them. Their Bengali-ness, then, does nothing for Bengali 'representation', because in any exaggeration, say drag, the job is not to affirm, but destabilize the idea of, say, being Bengali. This is also why I find his representation of the 'woman' so idealized, so entrenched in style and exaggeration, that it has nothing to do with women, at all.

In the present moment, Paro is being given the news by her ecstatic, screeching mother (Kirron Kher), that her longing bore fruit and that indeed, after a distance of a few oceans and a decade, Devdas is returning. Her mother understands that the longing for a childhood friend who left, through adolescence, becomes more potent, erotic, and unyielding. She seems to be the only adult in the room who does.

But this is not where Bhansali wants to grant us *darshan* of Paro. He is building tension as it rumbles towards that moment of grace. Darshan can be roughly translated as a sighting, but there is something seething under this neat, incomplete translation. To be sighted here is to be ritualized into existence. Much like *Chokkhu Daan* in West Bengal, where the statue of Durga, used during Durga Pooja, is given life by painting her eyes. There is no value to that statue, spiritually speaking, until this ritual confers it with both meaning, beauty, and, thus, existence.

In Bhansali's films, when lovers lay eyes on each other for the first time, or when the audience lays eyes on the characters, they are energized into being, a moment of grace. That, for him, is love.

Destiny is involved. When you are granted darshan, it is as though all of your life was meandering towards this very moment—a sacred, irresistible cliche. It is the romantic bulwark against any existential fugue that frustrates one's purpose in life.

Love at first sight liberally peppers Bhansali's filmography. When Raj (Salman Khan) lays eyes on Annie (Manisha Koirala) in *Khamoshi: The Musical* for the first time, it is his animated rite of passage into the film. In *Hum Dil De Chuke Sanam*, it is the fixed gaze of Nandini (Aishwarya Rai Bachchan) on Sameer (Salman Khan) when they first sight each other, a chandelier with candles swaying in between them, creating this ephemeral barrier between the two strangers who would, over the course of the next hour, be stained in each other's reckless love. Similarly, there is Ranbir Raj (Ranbir Kapoor) holding the gaze of Sakina (Sonam Kapoor) for the first time in *Saawariya* as she is running away from a drunk heckler; Ram (Ranveer Singh) fixated, hypnotized by Leela (Deepika Padukone) the first time their eyes cross paths in *Ram-Leela* amid a spray of Holi colours and a burst of bullets. Whether love at first sight is a human possibility, a biological lunge, or whether it is a mimetic aspiration we have inherited from cinema, it is an emotionally, erotically dense moment invoking, unrolling, predicting the intensity of the journey that the lovers will now chart.

This idea of darshan Bhansali takes to the logical, narrative, emotional, and erotic extreme in *Padmaavat* where Alauddin Khilji (Ranveer Singh), a brute, is willing to destroy a kingdom, deploy his army, devastate himself just to get a glimpse of Rani Padmavati (Deepika Padukone), whose unparalleled beauty he has only heard of; the things he does to merely get this darshan.

It makes sense, then, that in *Devdas*, Bhansali's cinematographer Binod Pradhan doesn't let us glimpse Paro immediately. We must grovel and wait. It is the sign of a devotee—an uneasy impatience, like a thronging crowd, early morning, waiting for the idol to be unveiled in temples. When we first hear her voice, reacting to her mother's news, Pradhan shoots it from the top, as though god—Bhansali's interpretation, not mine—is peering over this world pooling in the hued shadows of cut, coloured glass that make up the edifice of Paro's house. Then a shot from the side, with the lamp and Paro's arms in the foreground. Her friends—*sakhis*—attempt to blow this lamp, laughing at her longing, and failing to snuff it out. They begin to musically express this annoyance as an eyebrow knotting gesture. The lamp, like her desire, is headstrong, capable of, literally, braving fierce cloudbursts. It is only when the lightning ruptures the sky and the thunder breaks that we first see her face, illuminated in the sharp, ephemeral whiteness of that lightning, her metallic bindi reflecting that light as though it were lit from within, a magnesium circle burned hollow into her forehead. Her song begins. She is introduced through her perfumed, aching, gorgeous longing.

There are two other scenes with the cinematic force of an entry. When Devdas, as an adult, first meets Paro, for example. This is, technically, Devdas' introduction scene; it is when we first see his face as an adult, first lay eyes on Shah Rukh Khan. But Bhansali stages it as a breathless moment for Paro, shy of seeing Devdas, running away with alta still wet on her feet staining the floor, a flowing yellow sari whose loose end she pulls and then tosses over her shoulder as she gallops through corridors lined by partitions made from those very cut coloured glasses. For Bhansali, it is more important for us to see Paro as Devdas wants to than to see Devdas. Or perhaps, the joy of seeing Devdas has now been sublimated into the joy of seeing Devdas' love—an effacing of the self, expressed through the grammar of cinema.

Paro ends up, panting, on a bed, and uses the white sheet to shoo a bee that has disturbed her reverie. A choreography with thick, milk-white cloth ensues and it is in the fluster of this that we first see Devdas. Paro refuses to show her face to him. She is stretching that desperate moment waiting for darshan—of him for her, of her for him.

When she does show him her face, later, under the creaming moonlight, she makes her third, forceful, cinematic entrance. This scene serves as a masterclass in creating dynamism through stillness. When Bhansali wants to show time passing, the coloured shadows of the glass keep shifting—because of light shifting—as Devdas and Paro are stationary, invoking what writer Andre Aciman in *Call Me by Your Name* calls lovemaking, 'run[ning] circles around time'. Devdas is in thrall of Paro's face which is resting, in sleep. The camera moves vertically such that the focus remains on her face, and from behind them, the moon emerges into frame.

Even in *Hum Dil De Chuke Sanam,* being introduced to Nandini is like being introduced to a life force; excess distilled. Her walking on the *rann*, with the *kandeel*, a fluttering tinsel lantern crackling the soundscape, her *lehenga* with patches of metallic asparagus green and wine-drunk maroon, shimmering in the sun creating a thick watery haze of a mirage over which she is floating. A *chakda* comes along and she leaps onto it. If you pause your gaze, luring it towards the lehenga, you can see strains of peacock blue as the wind ripples through it and the sun spits its light. Through a frenzied song and dance around a game of *pitthu*—or seven stones, involving a ball and a pile of flat stones—she is allowed to bend into choreography, jumping, leaping, twisting her hips this way and that, in the spare, heat-domed Gujarati desert. It is a *gagging* celebration of her beauty.

Why is it that Bhansali generally prefers giving his women the introduction scene, as opposed to men who have, historically, crowded out this cinematic moment?

Perhaps because *shringaar* is essential to his women—the way Paro is applying alta on her feet when Devdas strikes at the door; the way Chandramukhi (Madhuri Dixit), the courtesan whom Devdas leans on after Paro gets married to someone else, is applying perfume when he is seeing her from the mirror—and shringaar is essential to his cinema, women are essential to his cinema in a way men just cannot be. The only way men can be celebrated is through their sexuality, their bare, hairless bodies, oiled, sculpted, and that is something he invokes strongly later in his filmography, with *Saawariya*, and then with a fuller, more muscular force in *Ram-Leela*. In both these films, *Ram-Leela* more specifically, we get that hero entry, full of boyish, acrobatic charm in the former, and irrepressible sex in the latter.

Besides, the surface of Bhansali's cinema is obsessed with movement—of fabric, of hair, of limbs. Women are able to conjure these flares, these dents in the space-time tissue of the film, slowing it down, spreading themselves out, with their bodies, their hair, their adornments, their clothing. Choreography is essential to his world—the way his characters walk, gesticulate, open letters, play games, and even eat, it is all coded to a *taal*.

His iconography is rooted in traditional ideas of being 'Indian'. The *sindoor* of a married woman, their *mangal-sutra*, the willing subservience of a wife to her husband, her touching of his feet, the reckless, relentless string of festivals that Bhansali milks for visual stimulus. Even the *kurta-pajama*, the *bandh-gala* he wore to Cannes for *Devdas*, did not feel like a statement as much as it was an effortless expression of his self. Bhansali, even to this day, can be seen in loose, black kurtas promoting his films, or on set.

He isn't a purist. In fact, he revels in what many might call cultural contaminations, insisting on, instead, the democratizing and popularizing of dance—folk and classical. He will get the Kathak exponent Birju Maharaj to choreograph a Kathak song in *Devdas* and *Bajirao Mastani* but he will also bring Saroj Khan and Remo D'Souza to choreograph songs, bringing in their trademark celluloid-tested-trusted thrusts and twirls that can be replicated. The best example of this synthesis, this radiant contamination is 'Ghoomar' from *Padmaavat*, which was choreographed both by Ghoomar exponent Jyothi Tommaar and Hindi cinema regular Kruti Mahesh, bringing in both the playfulness of folk tradition and the spice of cinema.

It is the 'spice' that he brings to cinema. Most of his films are based on raw material already available—mediaeval poetry, colonial literature, Russian short stories, Shakespeare, historical biographies, legends, novels, novellas, and even other films. His interpretation is adulterous, never faithful, adding scenes, editing out characters, swerving cinema to serve his autobiographical, aesthetic urges. Most of Bhansali's stories emerge from sources outside of him, and yet, he articulates, through them, the deeply personal nature of each film. In that sense, he is not really *creating* cinematic forms of thought as much as expanding them, exploding them.

The iconic, most cinematic representation of emotional masochism, the story of Devdas, the protagonist and title of the Bengali romance novel written by Sarat Chandra Chatterjee in 1917, found cinematic voice through P.C. Barua in the 1930s, Bimal Roy in 1955, and Bhansali in 2002. When Bhansali's film came out, there were over eight versions floating around already. Nasreen Munni Kabir in her book *Bollywood: The Indian Cinema Story*, notes how this story gave Hindi cinema its most enduring tropes—the love triangle; a man unable to fight the system; a sex worker with a heart of gold.

Cinematic regurgitations continued even after Bhansali, with Anurag Kashyap's psychedelic trance and Sudhir Mishra's small-town revisionism, among many others regularly littering the filmscape with their interpretations.

What is this singular fascination with a man so broken, and yet so ravishing that he has two decked, intelligent, and gorgeous women pine for him—Parvati or Paro, his childhood sweetheart who gets married to someone else and Chandramukhi, a courtesan in whose arms he turns a repentant alcoholic after Parvati leaves him? This is, undoubtedly, a male fantasy, and that it is men who pursue this story is telling; to be a brute, and to be loved, regardless.

Devdas does not marry Paro because her family comes from a lower rung of Brahmins. He does not fight his parents' will and prejudice, and this lax attitude comes back to haunt him as he drowns in alcoholism, placing a powder keg on his liver. The question of Devdas and Chandramukhi marrying is not even considered in the story. That he loves her, that he thinks of her, is enough for her to relinquish her courtesan life and become this pining devotee of Devdas. Bhansali, defending him, notes, '*Log kehte hai, yeh ek loser ki kahani hai. Main kehta hoon ki yeh greatest lover ki kahani hai.*'[1] People say this is the story of a loser, I say this is the story of the greatest lover.

This pining is inflected by Bhakti, which is a tradition strange to India, where from the sixth century in Tamil Nadu, thirteenth century in Maharashtra, and fifteenth and sixteenth century in North and East India, poets effaced themselves in devotion.

But who is this god that Mirabai, for example, in sixteenth century Rajasthan, submitted her life to, leaving her parents distraught and her in-laws frustrated?

Perhaps, the point of this devotion is not the god itself, but the devotee, and how despite being an idea, an idol, this god is capable of provoking poetry, love, speech, promises, and exalting breath. In Paro's devotion to Devdas, in Chandramukhi's devotion to Devdas, we don't see Devdas but these women in stronger light. As Amit Chaudhuri in his book *Finding the Raga: An Improvisation on Indian Music* writes, 'Bhakti isn't about god; it's about the impracticality and dignity of human emotion,' an impracticality and dignity—though I would argue, when lovesick, that it is indignity—Bhansali thickly applies over his seething, longing characters. That it is not Devdas as much as what Devdas evokes in the women that interests Bhansali. In some sense, Bhansali's filmography is an anthropomorphic extension of the Bhakti tradition, applying the human-god interaction to intra-human frisson.

Marriage, then, is a fascinating, almost irrelevant institution in Bhansali's films, much like marriage was useless in Krishna's world, with Radha, despite being married, falling in love with Krishna, who was already married to Rukmini.

For a man whose mainstay is love stories—or stories about love—marriage is entirely forgotten, as though he does not care for institutions that congeal love, as much as the contortions one must undergo to reach there, and to emerge from it. Or perhaps he isn't interested in marriage because he isn't interested in love as a linear journey with milestones that mark progress, as something sanctioned socially by the state, by the community. So, when lovers profess their love as though vows of marriage in *Hum Dil De Chuke Sanam* and *Bajirao Mastani*, it is done among the isolation of ruins, with just the lovers. He doesn't yoke love to marriage because marriage is destiny, sealed. That love is a reckless, unstable pursuit, just as amenable to collapse as it is to comfort, just as easily flared as it is extinguished.

In *Khamoshi: The Musical*—his first and only film where two people who love each other are shown getting married in a ceremony—Annie's parents don't show up for the church wedding, which has this incomplete, bittersweet sheen. It is clear that Bhansali sees the ritual marriage as merely social dance, not an intimate expression of long-pursued affections. This image of marriage curdles as his filmography progresses. Besides, marriage in cinema has always signalled a neat ending, almost as the collapse of destiny, beyond which nothing more needs to be known. Bhansali craves an aftermath in his movies, sniffing around for emotional irresponsibility.

In *Hum Dil De Chuke Sanam* and *Devdas*, the female protagonists get married to men they have no interest in or desire for, for their love resides elsewhere. In both cases, Aishwarya Rai Bachchan, with a blank expression of betrayal and existential ennui, sits on the wedding pedestal, broken. In *Devdas,* Paro's marriage to a richer zamindar is followed by her visiting Devdas' house, asking for his blessings, making sure he shoulders the palanquin on which she leaves for her in-laws. The song 'Hamesha Tumko Chaaha' plays in the background, a yanking reminder that her heart lurks elsewhere, and that marriage will do nothing to shift the shape and direction of that love. If anything, it will intensify it, such is the curse of a lover's absence.

Even in later films, Bhansali refuses to give into the ceremonial joy of marriage, the idealized notion of marriage in a love story as an inevitable destination with a treacherous path leading up to it. The purest expression of love is letting go of the lover, wishing them the best, as in *Saawariya* and *Gangubai Kathiawadi*, or to be willing to kill the man you love so he doesn't have to inhabit a disabled body so restlessly, as in *Guzaarish*, or to die together, pulse tied to pulse, as in *Ram-Leela* and *Bajirao Mastani*, and to kill oneself to uphold the honour of the lover, as in *Padmaavat*. There is something twisted, endlessly unfulfilled, about love. As though to love is to condemn yourself to eternal longing, or death.

There is something culturally troubling here, a belief that a story is of emotional and aesthetic value only if it is built on pain, on tragedy. That a story with neither pathos nor pain is not worthy. That you must suffer to be significant. This belief leaks beyond the seams of the film's frame. During the making of *Devdas*, fires were sweeping up sets, accidents were being reported, and the producer was in jail. The film was considered, by many, jinxed. Bhansali's response, in retrospect of course, was romance, 'We were all suffering. But out of the suffering I kept my vision alive. *Shayad Devdas ko sahi tarah se banane ke liye a state of mind bohut zaroori hai. Humko samajhna chahiye ki suffering kya hai, anguish kya hai.* We have to relate to the word pain in the correct sense of the word. *Jab tak hum us cheez se na guzre tab tak hume pata nahin chalega ki us cheez ko screen pe kaise translate kare.*'[2] That until you experience suffering, you can never express it on celluloid, truly. But suffering is not romantic when its sting doesn't elevate but cripples you. I read this quote to a friend who worked on and, anguished by the madness, left his set, her eyes rolling so far back in her head I thought she would trip backwards. Madness, sure, but where was the accountability? Madness, perhaps, cannot exist alongside accountability, and so when we are so ready to fetishize this artistic madness, we must hold alongside it, our indifference to accountability.

In 1998, cinema got 'industry' status, so finances were less dubious and production houses were peopled with corporate-types, and accountability became necessary. Insanity, in the corporate worldview, is the antithesis of accountability. This new formal ecosystem could never produce a filmmaker who would drag on shoots for months, refusing to show the film to producers, overshooting a budget, placing unreal demands on the artists working for him. *Devdas'* budget, at over 50 crore back in 2002, made it the most expensive Hindi film of that time—with over 260 shooting shifts stretched over two-and-a-half years; two crew members dying in accidents on set.

When it was time to shoot the climax of *Devdas*, the producer Bharat Shah was in jail. Bhansali used to spend time outside the jail hoping he would be released. The climax had Devdas holding onto his last breath as Paro runs furiously towards him, through the corridors of her marital home, reaching out, trying to hold him one last time. The budget permitted only one corridor, which they had first painted off-white. Then, on a whim, overnight Bhansali got it painted blue with Ajanta-Ellora motifs to make it look grander. And then the next night it was painted red. For the three days, Aishwarya Rai Bachchan kept running through the same corridor, as the film kept piling up.

While talking to the production designer Nitin Chandrakant Desai, he laughed at how things had to be scaled up. Paro's home in the film was made of 1.2 lakh pieces of stained glass at the cost Rs 3 crore. But since Devdas was higher on the caste and class ladder, his haveli had to be four times bigger, and so, they brought in scaffolding with over 128 columns, the first time such an endeavour was undertaken in Hindi cinema. These were merely two of six sets—the most expensive being Chandramukhi's kotha and the temple city around it, made at the cost of 12 crore. It was so large that you could walk two kilometers through it. Stories of the making of the film buzzed about like tabloid gossip, and members of the film fraternity would regularly show up just to see the set, as though a museum. The Maharashtra Governor P.C. Alexander even requested the director of Film City to retain Chandramukhi's kotha as a permanent tourist spot. Cinematographer Binod Pradhan had to use over 30 lakh watts of power from 42 generators to light these sets. Additional space had to be acquired at Film City just to park these generators. Marriages in Mumbai suffered because most of the generators were used in Film City.[3]

The demands he makes on his actors has plastered 'madness' onto his image—Madhuri Dixit Nene wearing a 30 kg *ghaghra* while dancing; the handcrafted Abu-Sandeep ghaghra that Dixit wore in *Devdas*, weighing 10 kgs, with mirrors embedded in zardozi, which took over two months to create; Aishwarya Rai Bachchan holding a pot on her head with one hand, standing on one leg, holding an increasingly heating up lantern with her other hand, a thorn on the sole of her other feet—a tradition of fetishizing the feet that goes back to *Pakeezah*

(1971) and *Salma* (1985), which Bhansali references again in *Heeramandi*. The beauty we see was now accompanied by this rich narrative of labour, of pain. That beauty is a project, an effort, a pulsing obsession. It can't *just* be made. It is often built on the carcass of human sweat.

When a set burns down, however, it is almost like a world collapsing. In February 2004, Bhansali was shooting in Film City for *Black*, his film after *Devdas*—which released to some withering critique at home and abroad regarding its melodrama, but was commercially successful. An ode to Helen Keller starring Rani Mukerji, all the equipment, lights, dolleys, and antique furniture he had borrowed had burned down. Something about lacquer being used to polish the floors and the lights being tripped. One of the biggest floors of Film City, 15,000 sq. feet, had crumbled to ash.

The set was built again with the noise of court cases buzzing around, from an art dealer from whom they borrowed furniture to Film City itself suing, and then, there was the ballooning budget. Since Bhansali wanted continuity, every item on set had to be replaced to look exactly like before the fire, down to the chairs, the paintings, and the chandeliers. Every night the set floor would be polished, and a white cloth would be placed on it.

~

From Bhansali's adaptation of Devdas' story—a process of extraction, elaboration, exaggeration, and ultimately exploration—we can understand the impulse of his cinema. Watching the film alongside its previous adaptations, seeing the spaces of emphasis, of retreating, of fabulation—

not only in the performances which are pitched a few thousand storeys higher, but also the circumstances—you can recognize what it is that Bhansali finds exciting and cinematic, and why it is that he was drawn to *this* story.

In Bimal Roy's version, Devdas walks into Chandramukhi's kotha the moment Paro walks into her marriage palanquin as parallel lunges of the respective bodies; Devdas is elsewhere. But Bhansali keeps Devdas close by, making his shoulder one of the many on which Paro's palanquin rests, giving their farewell this bleeding polish.

To see how Bhansali adapts Devdas is to see what it is about the story that attracted him to it. Bimal Roy's film is fairly straightforward. Devdas' mother rejects Paro's proposal entirely off-screen; this rejection is perfunctorily mentioned in a conversation between Devdas' parents. But when Bhansali hears about this exchange, he recognizes the potential for not just drama, but drama as expressed through musical howls and dramatic distortion—his answer to the singular question of how to infuse beauty into the story.

He concocts an elaborate scene. One where Paro's mother dances at Devdas's house to celebrate a child to be born in that house, followed by her proposal and its violent, dramatic, shattering rejection—a plate of vermilion, with a lamp, tossed away—which allows for one of the most poignant and melodramatic confrontations of Bhansali's filmography, where Paro's mother, humiliated, promises, in front of the thronging, spectatorial crowds, to have her daughter married to a house of higher station. A public rupture of dignity, a public show of courage, a public display of grace—these are moments Bhansali cannot resist. It allows for shame, and for power to cut through that shame and assert itself in an immediate, articulate, and cinematically satisfying way.

Bhansali intercuts this public theatre with a private one, with Paro and Devdas romancing by the moonlit waterfall, though romance is a light word for what is happening. As they walk across grass, Paro's feet are punctured by a thorn, her sole bleeding. As she reaches out to pluck it from her skin—bending her knees backwards and twisting her body to reach out—Devdas swats her hands. That only he has the right to draw blood from her, such is his grotesque, total sense of ownership. This is sex, make no mistake of the penetrative thorn's presence. This is domination. He unplucks the thorn and kisses the wound as Paro is balancing a pot of water on her head.

What Bhansali has done is elaborate the story, introduce characters bursting with intention—like Paro's mother, Devdas' mother—who were left hazily sketched in a previous iteration. Bimal Roy's storytelling is more focused, in that sense. It isn't even interested in establishing the love between Devdas and Paro as much as it is in establishing its violence. Bhansali wants us to see the love in the violence, the beating heart in the grasping hand. Bhansali's Devdas is far more in love with Paro. Or at least his possessiveness is far more grounded in what he calls love.

So, while Roy spends a longer time luxuriating in Devdas and Paro's childhood, Bhansali keeps them as peripheral jots, quick, efficient flashbacks—efficient, a word you would never otherwise use to describe Bhansali's art. There is no drama there to milk except that of Paro seeing Devdas leave. Roy uses *baul* music to verbalize what is happening in the heart of young Paro. Bhansali prefers his characters to do that themselves. Even a small gesture in Roy's film—Paro and Chandramukhi passing each other, for example—is in Bhansali's hands an enormous patch of mud that he sculpts into one song, one confrontation, and one moment of feminine companionship. He also bestows a distinct materiality to the film—concrete to Devdas, glass to Paro, mirrors to Chandramukhi.

Bhansali couldn't care less for literary accuracy. He barely thinks of historic accuracy, the way he made Kashibai (Priyanka Chopra Jonas) and Mastani (Deepika Padukone)—the two lovers of Bajirao, the eighteenth century Maratha Peshwa, who according to historic records never met—meet, feud, dance, and dulcet in *Bajirao Mastani*.

Bhansali is interested in something beyond 'truth' or 'authenticity', he is instead chasing both nostalgia and mythology. It is the devotion with which Paro holds Devdas' love over the years that he is fascinated by. He uses the lamp which she keeps lit in his memory as that symbol. It's grand and beautiful, amenable to music, drama, and dialogue.

This is because, based on his interviews, he sees in Devdas a reflection of his father—Navin Bhansali, who drowned in debt and alcohol after losing all his money on the few B-grade films he produced, like *Jahazi Lootera* (1953). Every Bhansali film is an offering to his father, each film beginning with a dedication to him, but *Devdas* especially so. It is almost pathetic, poignant, this pleading for his affection. (*Jahazi Lootera* even gets a shoutout in *Gangubai Kathiawadi,* where a poster of it is seen outside the theatre in the film, set in the 1950s.)

In Bhansali's narration of his life, his mercurial father, who died of cirrhosis, in his final moments came out of his coma and extended his hand towards his mother, a gesture that Devdas, too, performs in his final moments in the film, at the entrance of Paro's marital home. Trauma became grist in Bhansali's hands. He would, in interviews promoting his films, invoke his life.

There is a fascinating thesis, one that you must take with a grain of salt—that Bhansali's cinema must be read alongside that of Karan Johar and Aditya Chopra, that brewed into life in the same decade of the 1990s, to discern its true value and intention. While Johar and Chopra had widened the cinematic canvas, catering to the NRI audience, requiring a suspension of audience disbelief in order to give them ideals of being a modern Indian—by being both modern and Indian, with one's modernity not exerting itself forcefully on one's mehendi, Bhangra, and 'Om Jai Jagdish Hare', and one's Indianness not crowding out the leather jackets, DKNY shirts, and tight jeans—Bhansali's canvas decided to go a more traditional route.

Post the 1991 liberalization of the Indian economy, with the infusion of cultural edicts like Channel V and Star, while the audience was looking for a cinema that allowed for the Westernized Indian to take shape, many were also looking for a more revivalist, rooted Indian ideal to grasp and fashion themselves in the reflection of. Bhansali's cinema, according to this thesis, sated that appetite. Like how, in the face of Company Paintings of the British Raj which funnelled into the Bombay School, the Calcutta painters, in the nineteenth century, decided to do a revivalist style of painting, looking into their past and pulling folk art and Hindu imagery back to the foreground as an intentional, intense praxis. The Tagores were instrumental in this pursuit. This revivalism is considered an integral aspect of what we call Indian Modernism—to move ahead is to look back, to convert past heritage into contemporary tradition.

In this context, Bhansali's cinema can be seen as a stab at revivalism. His meticulously choreographed music numbers provide a roadmap as we attempt this argument—bringing in Kathak and Garba, Saroj Khan-ing them into a pulpy pit of revelry. In the '90s, with the MTV-fication of the media, the dance sequences got glossier, the background dancers svelte, the apparel hipper, the edits quicker, and then quicker, still more, with the fading of film into digital. Choreographers like Shiamak Davar and Farah Khan ushered in a new way of conceiving choreography, and were becoming household names because of their appearance on dance reality shows, garnering a fanbase of their own. Unlike classical dance which resists authorship, this contemporary form was congealing on styles, and styles on choreographer-celebrities.

Many dismissed these trends—Vyjayanthimala saying that it was the camera that is 'do[ing] all the dancing'; Helen calling it 'gymnastics'[4]—mourning the loss of performance in dance, ceding that territory to flashy acrobatics, to bonelessness. The way Bhansali stages a song becomes, then, a tether to a previous generation of filmmaking, where the songs were a saucy space for nakhra, for grace, not callisthenics.

Why, then, am I telling you to take this argument with a grain of salt?

Because, for one, Bhansali toes no line but his own, which zigzags, out of tune. After *Devdas*, he would make *Black*, mostly steeped in English, colonial iconography, English poetry, without any music, and very little colour. He would rope in Shiamak Davar—that very patron saint of dance from the 'West'—later, for *Saawariya,* and Vishnu Deva for *Ram-Leela*, before returning to the traditionalists. His films refuse to be slotted comfortably into arguments; they wiggle around.

But, also, unlike Chopra and Johar's cinema, there was *nothing* aspirational about Bhansali's cinema. He never created characters whom you want to emulate, so full of grief, so torn by life, so wrecked by exaggeration they were. Even if he created riotous ponds of culture and festivities, he bore them down with gruelling patriarchy. There were no malls, no Eurorails, no Switzerland, no London, no marriages. Even as the Johars and Chopras were weaving their dreams, they grounded much of it in the world we can recognize, a realism and a progressive lunge, even if it was illusory.

Bhansali was also not consciously adopting the Indian approach to cinema. It was what he understood best. His was a blind pursuit of shringaar, burnished by the cinema of Guru Dutt, K. Asif, Kamal Amrohi, and V. Shantaram. He sees his cinema as a continuation of *that* tradition, almost like he skipped the cinema of the '80s, '90s in his head.

His films are peppered with references to these older films, and nowhere is this more apparent than in *Bajirao Mastani* where the song 'Mohe Rang Do Laal' paid an ode to *Mughal-e-Azam's* 'Mohe Panghat Pe', the Aaina Mahal made in the shadow of *Mughal-e-Azam's* Sheesh Mahal, the 'Latpat Latpat' opening of 'Pinga' being a tribute to 'Latpat Latpat Tujha Chaalan Ga' sung by Lata Mangeshkar for V. Shantaram's *Amar Bhoopali*, or even the image of a woman blowing a *sringa*, used in both the logo of V Shantaram's Prabhat Film Company and the opening image of the song 'Albela Sajan'. Elsewhere, it is the mere shadow of these films, filmmakers, and actors which fall on Bhansali's art, their names being invoked as vague references, as moods, vibes.

Even today, in interviews, you get the sense that he does not watch many contemporary movies, floating above them. Though, he does go ahead and produce a film like Prabhu Deva's deafening, hip-pinching romp *Rowdy Rathore*, which was like the 'film[s] I used to clap and cheer for as a child at Alankar Talkies and Imperial Talkies alike,'[5] which speaks to the selective parts of his personality he wants to tease out through his direction.

While it is an interesting way to think of Bhansali's cinema alongside Johar's Dharma Productions and Chopra's Yash Raj Films, Bhansali never saw himself in opposition to anything. His cinema never seemed reactionary, just that he was innately drawn to and obsessed with stories and legends for years, stories which preceded independent India by decades, sometimes centuries. The story of *Bajirao Mastani*, for example, was with him for over a decade, and it took twelve years and three failed attempts before he finally cracked the cast. Over these twelve years, there was a genre shift in Hindi cinema from romance to rogue, with a new generation of actors crowding out an older lot, but Bhansali's vision doesn't seem to have been made malleable by time.

It was also the rigour and mythical weight of K. Asif that Bhansali gravitated towards—slaving over eight years to make *Mughal-e-Azam*, what critic Anupama Chopra called an 'insane, all-consuming passion that drives ordinary men to do extraordinary things'[6], something that had leaked out of Hindi cinema in the twenty-first century. As critic Leo

Robson wrote of Wes Anderson, with Bhansali, too, 'the mutation of the director's taste for tweaking the world into a need to rebuild it from scratch [is] an imperial-utopian project that extends far beyond the realm of typography and decor.'[7]

Devdas was, largely, a hermetically sealed, pedantically constructed world, with few peeks of the outside world existing. It is this elaborate, excessive, egregious control over the world that allowed him to fixate, luxuriate, and pontificate on beauty with more clarity and a celebratory zeal. Think of the introduction of two heroines—Nandini in *Hum Dil De Chuke Sanam* (1999) and Leela in *Ram-Leela* (2013), both set in the rann of Gujarat, both involving them running in flowing ghaghras, Neeta Lulla and Anju Modi respectively. While Nandini was running in the actual Rann, lensed by Anil Mehta, whose frames seem more comfortable in natural light than sets, Leela was running in a set bursting with colour, lensed by Ravi Varman whose frames are exhilarated by choreographed colour. The intense control of the scene—the slow-motion, the way the extras are postured and positioned at the bottom of the frame, all dunked in copper sulphate blue, looking like a border to the frame—allows the beauty to emerge more easily to the surface. *Devdas*, under the careful lensing of Binod Pradhan, was that inflection point, towards a more governed gorgeousness, a beauty that is produced invasively, intensely, what Robson calls 'a storm in a snow globe'. From here, he would move towards cinematographer Ravi K. Chandran's chiaroscuro compositions in *Black* and *Saawariya*, more dramatic, with shadows exerting a cinematic pressure on the image, and even on the psychology of characters.

The music of this snow globe was part of its storm, too. From his debut, Bhansali's seduction by and importance to music was clear when he insisted on Jatin and Lalit to compose, who were cresting at the height of their career with *Dilwale Dulhania Le Jayenge*, and Majrooh Sultanpuri as lyricist—who has written lyrics for directors like Guru Dutt and Mehboob Khan, whose Urdu has been cushioning the tunes, from the late '40s, of Naushad, Ghulam Mohammed, Madan Mohan, O.P. Nayyar, Roshan, Kalyanji–Anandji, Laxmikant–Pyarelal, and R.D. Burman.

But Bhansali never let his artists rest on their laurels. The Urdu poet from the Progressive Writers' Movement was folding English into Urdu in lyrics like 'Tell Me O Khuda', and his composers were cobbling songs which had a fourteen-line mukhda. 'Jaana suno hum tum par marte hain' . . . would start right from the lower note. Slowly the orchestra grows, then it goes very high with the full orchestra, brass and everything. I had never done anything like that before and I've never done anything like that since,'[8] Lalit notes.

Ismail Darbar, who was a violinist with Jatin–Lalit—he learned the violin from the father of Pyarelal from the famed Laxmikant–Pyarelal duo, when he moved from Surat to then-Bombay with his father—composed the music for *Hum Dil De Chuke Sanam*, his debut as a composer, and *Devdas*. It was in this latter album, with lyrics penned by Nusrat Badr, that Shreya Ghoshal got her break as a singer—Bhansali's mother was struck by her voice, watching her as a participant in *Sa Re Ga Ma* while she was singing a bhajan of Lata Mangeshkar.

One of the things that made *Devdas* dye in cinematic memory is its soundscape designed by Monty Sharma, who would go onto compose his first album with *Saawariya*. The film begins with an image of Durga and the sound of cymbals, bells, and women ululating, an 'ooli'—the sound is a high-pitched shriek of wind, cut by the rapid back and forth of the tongue fluttering like a demented wiper blade.

Then, suddenly, as if you were dropped from a height, producing a sharp needle up the nose, the pungent sound settles into soft hums, tinkles, and anklets, with the names 'Shahrukh Khan', 'Madhuri Dixit', and 'Aishwarya Rai' against the backdrop of a vermillion red carpet and watery impressions of Ajanta murals emerging from it, murals which art critic Stella Kramrisch described, as 'a gale of stillness'; with violins and a classical alaap orchestrally swelling into a crescendo as the film's title appears, punctuated by the ominous, shattering noise of lightning. *Devdas* has arrived.

When I spoke to the composer Monty Sharma, he was clear about how important it is to build, from the very beginning, a sense of awe, 'If I can create goose bumps right at the start of the film, it will make the whole thing magical.' When *Saawariya* begins, too, we have this strange, deep sound, as though we were in an aeroplane cabin up in the sky, a feeling of being sealed, suspended.

After three years of shooting, compiling, and editing the footage of *Devdas* into a raw cut, Bhansali came to Sharma, asking him to compose the background score. They had previously worked on *Hum Dil De Chuke Sanam*, for which Sharma had arranged the music. This would be the first time Monty Sharma—nephew of Pyarelal Ramprasad Sharma of the Laxmikant–Pyarelal duo, who began his journey playing the keyboard in *Mr. India* as a teenager—was composing the score for a big film. The next six months were spent feeling and evoking rapture through music; girding, emphasizing, and propelling the exquisite and emotionally exhausting melodrama of the three-hour long film.

There were no references, no odes to pay that he had in mind. The music simply emerged. Like Tipu Sultan archiving his dreams, Monty Sharma would wake up having dreamt of a tune and diligently note the notations—to bring what was in his head in front of his eyes.

An imprecise, intuitive combination of Indian and Western music, there were lots of strings, the cello along with the Indian flute; percussion and rhythms by Taufiq Qureshi, tabla maestro Zakir Hussain's younger brother. For some scenes, Sharma demanded ten tablas, with chorus sections of over forty singers, six female and six male classical singers, including green talent like Parthiv Gohil and Javed Ali, who would go on to chart their respective successful playback careers, mostly tethered to Bhansali's albums.

There were 250 artists playing instruments for the score of *Devdas*. While music programmers only used violins, Sharma used violins, violas, cellos, and the double bass to slather a moment with different frequencies, producing a richness of sound that is rare in Indian background music. Bhansali gave in to all his demands.

Sharma pursued his experiments and intuitions with sound, fusion, cyclical beats and layering. So, '*jaise langda aadmi ka chalan alag hota hai*', like a limp man walks differently, Sharma used 4.5 beats as the cyclical base for the opening credits song, as opposed to the more common four-beat cycle, creating a slight disorientation at the very outset of the film.

One of the striking aspects of Devdas's background score is the presence of voices and the silken chorus where usually musical instruments suffice; a spectral presence of voices in the score, Geetika Varde Qureshi's voice, for example, in the background when Paro and Devdas first meet as adults. Like a halo, as though the drama was being watched from above, an aural equivalent of Gustav Klimt's gilded choir of angels watching over the embracing couple in the *Beethoven Frieze*, the lovers in erotic embrace.

For the climax, Sharma was desperately looking for 'a musical storm' to elevate the cinematic swell of Paro's run towards Devdas who is inching towards death. He asked the Bengalis he knew what they would say if their heart was weeping. The singer Supriya Adhikari, a Bengali herself, suggested, '*Mon amar mon, aaye re mon, kaande amar mon*', O my heart, my weeping heart, a yearning plea that Sharma used, softly fitting the words to the melody he had already composed. Because this wail had to be sung at a high pitch, it was sung in piecemeal chunks.

There is an apparent, almost obvious reason *Devdas* ranks among the finest Indian films made, certainly the finest of Bhansali. You emerge from it after having the wind knocked out of your body, recovering from a climax so crowded with Sharma's sound and fury, Binod Pradhan's sweeping camera, and the fluttering costume design, that there isn't space for anything but sublimated submission, one that I keep coming back to like a prayer.

Saawariya, Doused in Blues

Daras bina nahin chain

No darshan, no relief.

—Sameer

At the height of his career—or one of the many heights of his long, ongoing career—with the French buzz around the riotous *Devdas* and the near-universal critical acclaim of the subdued *Black* in India, the god complex that every director harbours—must harbour, in fact—infected Bhansali with a strange, full-bodied extravagance.

His next film, *Saawariya*, based on Russian novelist Fyodor Dostoevsky's 1848 short story *White Nights*, would star rank newcomers—Sonam Kapoor (the daughter of Anil Kapoor) and Ranbir Kapoor (the scion of the Kapoor *khandaan*, son of Rishi Kapoor and Neetu Kapoor), both of whom assisted Bhansali on *Black*.

Most directors have this moment in their career when they jump off a cliff, having worked with established actors, to mentor newer ones. Raj Kapoor did it in *Bobby* (1973), Karan Johar did it in *Student of The Year* (2012), Mani Ratnam did it in *Kadal* (2013), Zoya Akhtar did it in *The Archies* (2023). To work with actors versus to sculpt them, this is the distinction here; that until now their contribution to cinema has been their art, and now, artists, too.

If you are pliable to a little naughty psychoanalysis, it can also be read as a moment where a filmmaker is trying to pursue a younger subculture in their work, their art, and through their art, perhaps, their life—all the above directors made their respective films in their forties to early fifties.

The story of *Saawariya* takes place over four nights. On the first night, Ranbir Raj (Ranbir Kapoor) lays eyes on Sakina (Sonam Kapoor) who is mysteriously waiting on a bridge. Raj is smitten; Sakina is cold.

On the second night, she narrates to him the reason for her being perched on a bridge on a night so cold—she is waiting for her lover, Iman (Salman Khan), who left the previous year, promising he would be back by Eid this year. She gives Raj a letter to post to Iman. Raj agrees, moping. Later, in jealousy, he burns the letter.

The third night, he sees her from a distance, guilty of his offence. But then, as an expiation, he personally goes to the address of the letter to deliver its message in person, only to find out no such Iman exists, and that perhaps Sakina is fooling him. He is overjoyed. Sakina is his.

The fourth night, the night of Eid, he would perform for her his feelings and marry her.

Sakina, too, by now has started losing hope that Iman will return. A strange imbalance enters the film, where Raj thinks Iman does not exist, but Sakina, who believes Iman exists, is losing her grip over that lover's conviction. She relents, slightly, cozying into Raj's arms, then slightly, some more, only for Raj's hopes to be dashed in a climactic moment, when Iman is finally seen on the bridge. Sakina asks for both Raj's forgiveness and blessings, and he wishes her farewell, smiling through his heartbreak.

Dostoevsky's text is a study of urban loneliness. The main protagonist, who calls himself the 'Dreamer', drowning in his own daydreams, floats around the city, a man with no history, no future, like Godard's fictional children. He has no companion, no acquaintance to breeze his life past, and no one to breeze their lives past him.

Love enters his life like a moment of grace. While she is burdened by history, he is full of only dreams. It is her backstory that is delved into, not his, taking us back to the idea that women in Bhansali's films tend to have pasts, which they needle at through flashbacks, but the men simply appear, as if etherized into being.

When this love leaves, it stains his life, but there is no rancour. This is the abiding principle of loving and not being loved in Bhansali's world—to feel broken, beaten, but never bitter.

From Sameer in *Hum Dil De Chuke Sanam*, Chandramukhi in *Devdas*, Kashibai in *Bajirao Mastani*, and even Gangubai in *Gangubai Kathiawadi* renouncing her love, Bhansali is fixated on the idea of love as sacrifice, a pious act of painful withdrawal, an eventual ambivalence towards the idea of possession—that to be in love, you must merely *be*, not *have*. Its most powerful incarnation is in *Guzaarish*, where Sofia (Aishwarya Rai Bachchan), the nurse to the paraplegic Ethan (Hrithik Roshan), is willing to kill him after the courts reject his mercy killing petition. She loves him so much, she will extinguish him, for that is what he wants, her demands taking the shape of his.

You can ask, what is it about a paraplegic has-been that evokes so much love in this gorgeous woman, that she is willing to set her life aside for him? All descendants of the French philosopher Roland Barthes' conception of love in *A Lover's Discourse* (1977), they believe in the following.

'Love illuminates for us our imperfection. It is nothing other than the uncanny movement of our consciousness comparing two unequal terms—on the one hand, all the perfection and plenitude of the beloved; on the other hand, all the misery, thirst, and destitution of ourselves—and the fierce desire to unite these two such disparate terms.' [1]

That to love is to feel, fiercely, your inadequacy against the abundance of the lover, irrespective of who they are, how they look, what they earn. To then look at their resplendence and ask them to do better, find better, is to speak against the language of love. To look at Chandramukhi and insist that she can do better than Devdas is to disrespect the very curdled, cursive logic—if you can even call it that, an anti-logic, perhaps—of loving. As Gillian Rose writes in her fragile memoir *Love's Work*, 'There is no democracy in any love relation: only mercy.'[2]

What sets *Saawariya* apart from this asymmetry is the innocence that Bhansali inflects pathos with. Ranbir Raj is still a boy, airdropped from some strange, ill-fitted imagination. In 'Jab Se Tere Naina', excited by new love, half-naked in his own solitude—his butt was censored off, the cut coming right as the towel drops—he flails in abandon, singing and dancing, making eye contact with us, directly, drawing us into his bursting, bubbling heart. This direct gaze, what film theorists call the breaking of the fourth wall—look at the choice of violent words, 'breaking', 'wall' assuming this distance from the screen, with the 'wall' having a strangely sinister sieving interpretation in a post-Trump world—was deployed earlier by Bhansali, in another moment of innocent euphoria, in 'Aaj Mein Upar' from *Khamoshi: The Musical*, when Annie is dancing by herself, seemingly alone in the house. It almost feels like a private performance, but the way she keeps glimpsing at the camera, the way he keeps glimpsing at the camera, at us, there is this heady sense that we, too, are part of their solitude.

In Amit Chaudhuri's book *Finding the Raga: An Improvisation on Indian Music*, he speaks of an argument he had with an older man, when Chaudhuri was younger, regarding William Blake's *Songs of Innocence and Experience*. Chaudhuri was convinced that despite coming chronologically first, the songs of innocence were written after the songs of experience. (This is not true, and Chaudhuri knows this, but he persists, hungering over a hunch). He says, in that throwaway philosophical naivete of youth, 'You only arrive at the simplicity and calm of innocence *after* experience, not before it,' that innocence is borne out of experience, not preceding it.[3]

A strange theory, one that sees Raj in Bhansali's filmography as not an airy blank slate, unwritten on, but as someone who was birthed from the pathos of Sameer's heartbreak in *Hum Dil De Chuke Sanam* and Devdas sowing his life with landmines. It flips the way we think of Raj—not as someone who is yet to be blemished, but as someone, who having experienced the blemishing, emerged unstained.

Raj has keys dangling from his body but no place to go. He refuses to fold both his sleeves, he buttons up only the holes he wishes to seal, sometimes just one, often more, once the only button that is closed is the one of the collars, the shirt fluttering about, giving sheepish glimpses of his sculpted body. He romances a tissued curtain with Mona Lisa painted on it, him shirtless. By romance, I mean flinging his arms as the curtain flutters onto his body; a dance of rapture that comes from the silken touch of skin against woven air. As Barthes writes, 'Every contact, for the lover, raises the question of an answer: the skin is asked to reply.'

Ranbir's body for the film is chiselled, but not pumped, his arms tight but not bulging, a *taweez*-like thread curled around his right bicep, an earring on his left lobe. The image is not of hulking masculinity, but something softer, even if it is forged into being in the gym. You cannot not see the labour that went into the sculpting, the saltless hours, waterless days that shrink the skin to meet the ripped muscle.

The year of Saawariya's release was seminal, for the man's body was now being articulated in popular culture in a particular, distinct way that would leave its imprint on Hindi cinema. This masculine body has often been a site to inscribe desire—desire to be the body, desire to be *with* the body. The queerness of it cannot be overstated, where both the desire to be and be with were mingling inextricably.

The 'men's physique' magazines in the 1950s and '60s USA, for example, were a space for producing softcore porn, disguising homoerotic desire as bodybuilding, avoiding the moral censure of the censors. This explains how a gay photographer, filmmaker, and later pornographer, James Bidgood, cut his teeth in magazines like *Muscleboy*, *The Young Physique*, and *Demi Gods*. It is desire that drives these images. It is also why these magazines would later go to great lengths to heterosexualize the muscle by adding women models on the side, dictating whose gaze the muscles are meant for.

In India, this took more time. Michiel Baas in his book *Muscular India: Masculinity, Mobility & The New Middle Class* argues, 'The lean, muscular, ideal body type has emerged among middle-class Indian men'[4] only in the last decade. Based on interviews with bodybuilders, he credits *Om Shanti Om*—which released on the same day as *Saawariya*, burying it under its success—and Shah Rukh Khan's 'freshly baked abs' unveiled in the satirical item song 'Dard-e-disco' as a culturally formative moment for masculinity in India. This was bolstered by *Men's Health* magazine which launched its Indian edition the same year, platforming ripped non-celebrities as cover models. There was, he argues, a sudden spurt in gym memberships. The release of Aamir Khan's *Ghajini* the following year gave this leaf-turning further momentum. As masculinities were becoming more and more deep-set, the abs iron-clad, the biceps rippling, *Saawariya* existed as a softer, more playful alternative, even as it insisted on the body being shapely and hairless. Watching how Ranbir dances throughout the film, a footloose, chaotic flailing, where every exaggerated movement is an expression of his exaggerated passion, is to place your finger on a moment where Bhansali both bolstered and bucked a trend.

For a second now, just a second, let us fixate on the hair sprouting on Kapoor's body. In his second film, *Bachna Ae Haseeno*, Kapoor would continue his svelte shirtless schtick, but this time, there is armpit hair. Shaved underarms, as Shannon Philip, postdoctoral researcher at the Department of Sociology, University Of Cambridge argues in his book *Becoming Young Men In A New India: Masculinities, Gender Relations and Violence in the Postcolony* argues, was part of a new commodified masculinity that was gripping the young male, with many spending money on body-hair removal products—out of ideas of cleanliness, but also aesthetics, but also, strangely, visibility; to be able to see the flexed parts of the body unclouded by thick clods of hair.[5]

A decade and a half later, over the course of which Kapoor perfected the metrosexual hairless man, punctured here and there by hairy rebels and Punjabi shrubs, in the most successful film of his career, *Animal* (2023)—inflected heavily by the traditions of Telugu cinema that brewed its director Sandeep Reddy Vanga—hair on the body, like an evening shadow, would be accompanied by dialogue that promotes keeping pubic hair. Kapoor, arcing through his filmography, has charted the psyche, both aspirational and relatable, of the Indian male—the playboy in *Bachna Ae Haseeno* (2008), the entrepreneurial bug in *Rocket Singh* (2009), the rebel in *Rockstar* (2011), struck by wanderlust in *Yeh Jawani Hai Deewani* (2013), existential ennui in *Tamasha* (2015), etc. For him, to then swerve away from the smoothed hairlessness of his debut, is to both construct and consecrate a strain of thought among men and their idealized aesthetics.

I wonder though, how to place Bhansali's hairless—body hair, that is—heroes? Ranveer Singh's polished, ab-poked skin in *Ram-Leela*, *Bajirao Mastani*, and *Padmaavat* (in the last, he was afforded sparse sproutings of chest hair) and Shahid Kapoor's svelte body bleached of fat and hair in *Padmaavat*, fall in line with Ranbir Kapoor, and before him, that of Salman Khan's—a *silsila* of hairless bodies, waxed armpits, chiselled torsos. Here is an inability to see the hairy body as a site of erotic desire, of the limits Bhansali places on the sexualized masculinity of his characters.

~

Getting the studio floors warmed and sputtering for *Saawariya*, Bhansali reached out to Kathak exponent Uma Dogra. He wanted Sonam Kapoor to train under her, not to make her a dancer, as much as to make her inhabit the dancer's body, that innate sense of grace, that precision in the poise. He envisioned *Saawariya* as a painting whose colour keeps leaking into shapes, as that terribly overused pithy phrase, 'poetry in motion'. Bhansali would sit in on Dogra's classes with Sonam Kapoor, for two hours, every day, over three months, looking at how his creation was shaping up. Bhansali is intensely aware of the body, its frame. In the video on the film's making, you can hear him talking to the costume designer of the film, the couturier Anuradha Vakil, telling her how a certain length of the lehenga looks 'clumsy' on Kapoor because she has 'the same structural problem' as Tabu and Nutan, that is, she shoots up into the sky with her height.[6]

Bhansali insisted that when Kapoor runs in this film, it must look like a dancer is running. 'We get so many requests to train people because they want to learn rhythm. But he asked for grace. The person he had in mind was Waheeda Rehman,' Dogra told Film Companion.

Grace, like perfume, is emitted from the body, incapable of being bottled up and replicated, concentrated in gestures. Edmund Burke, the eighteenth century Anglo-Irish philosopher, in his treatise, *A Philosophical Enquiry into the Origins of the Sublime and Beautiful*, thinks of grace as something more specific than beauty, that it can belong to both 'posture and motion', that 'it is requisite that there be no appearance of difficulty... [not] to appear divided by sharp and sudden angles', that is must have 'this ease, this roundness, this delicacy of attitude and motion.'[7]

In *Saawariya*, for example, Bhansali keeps making Sakina freeze in postures, to amber in motion, stillness. When she gives her hand to Raj in a gesture of friendship, a handshake, she holds the pose mid-air, even when Raj has extricated his hand from the shake—suspended, her long fingers curling slightly. As though every limbic permutation is conscious of it being an act of hewing space, cutting through air, making it malleable, hollowed, with the body's force.

So conscious of this body that it forgets the things it holds, that it is adorned by. Sakina keeps dropping items, leaving them behind for Raj to collect—when her hand is mid-air, and she is slinking away, the shawl resting on her arm gets caught in a door's handle; her umbrella; her anklets. This forgetfulness, thoughtlessness, is seen by Bhansali as an exercise in grace; to be so embedded in your body, nothing else matters.

Both Ranbir Kapoor and Sonam Kapoor spent nine months being groomed by Bhansali, reading and rereading scripts of other films, performing to music, dancing together, making fools of themselves, building and cementing chemistry and innocence—ah, here again, Amit Chaudhuri's theory that innocence is not something you emerge out of, but labour into. There is a sweet video somewhere on the internet of the two of them lip-syncing to the song 'My Dil Goes Mmmm' from *Salaam Namaste* (2005), miming being on a bike, unravelling in giggles. They did over twenty photoshoots to figure out their angles, what works, what doesn't. 'With Sonam, surprisingly, every angle worked,' Bhansali notes.

The decision was made that the film would be shot *entirely* indoors, around ten sets. Cinematographer Ravi K. Chandran had worked with Bhansali earlier on *Black*. That was the first time they were attempting Digital Intermediate (DI), scanning negatives, making it digital, cleaning the frames, then printing it back into film. This helped filmmakers tweak light and colour. For *Saawariya*, he got Spacelights from the USA to provide that soft overhead lighting, which he gelled blue for a coolness in the image. They were looking at paintings of Frederick Arthur Bridgman and his eye for the 'Oriental', lounging exotic, Fred R. Wagner's thick impressionism, and the landscape painter William Louis Sonntag's serene snapshots of lakes and mountain sides.

Nothing would look real. The maximalist irreality of this world—where Venice, the 'Orient', the dyed walls of Chefchaouen, the reckless Kamathipura, and studied Lucknow emerge side-by-side, with colonial clock towers and Bamiyan-sized Buddhist statues, murals of Lakshmi, classical Greek sculptures, and Urdu calligraphy, where you call your lover the Arabic-origin 'saba' or morning breeze right before calling her the Sanskrit-origin 'ghataa' or a handful of clouds—need not be explained, save for a gesture at the beginning of the film, when the narrator, the sex worker Gulab-ji (Rani Mukerji) calls it a 'khwabon ka sheher', a city of dreams, before she invites us into her narration of the life of a special someone who walked into this city and her life one day, her Saawariya—meaning beloved, meaning Krishna, the dark one, ironic, given Ranbir's milk-struck complexion—Ranbir Raj.

How do we consume a dream, then? It is airy, without foundation or being. Like a mirage, it shimmers its possibilities, always eluding your grasp of it.

Nothing else about this world and nobody in it explains its ghostly, suspended existence, the logic of its weather—snowy, rainy, windy—or its history—wars and barracks, populated mostly by women—or its place in the world. Suspended in some half-formed state, the world-building kept pushing the limits of artifice. In the song 'Pari', where Ranbir Raj is serenading street sex workers—mostly aged, smoking, coughing, bruised, cackling—in the indigo night, there are sometimes patches of harsh afternoon light that fall on their faces. Are these street lamps or a schizophrenic sun that ruptures the surface of the film every now and then? Sakina, when narrating her past, her love for Iman, speaks of a night where she went to his bedroom, but the light we see falling on his face is the shadowless, white, noontime heat. Later, they are on the bed, sleeping together, and the light feels like a golden dawn ripped through.

One of the words for cinematography in Tamil is known as *olipathivu*, literally 'an impression of light'. This phrasing seems to give power to 'light'—that light produces an impression, as opposed to light allowing something else to produce an impression. Modern cinematography in studios, however, is not interested in the impression of light as opposed to the capturing of it, a mastery over it, a terrible control which creates a templated, algorithmic, predictable, charmless deploying of the very thing that makes cinema possible—light. Not Bhansali, and certainly not in *Saawariya*.

Let me, then, direct your salivating attention to Ranbir Kapoor's back, the ravines of taut muscle.

When 'Jab Se Tere Naina' begins, Raj is standing with only his white towel at his window—the panes wet with condensation—against a shop's name, its letters lit up with bulbs, the light alternating among the letters. A nod to both his father, Rishi Kapoor's infamous towel-dropping, booty-popping moment in his debut film, *Bobby* (1973) and Kajol's towel dance in *Dilwale Dulhaniya Le Jayenge* (1995), the whiteness of the towel, here, elevates these references to Bhansali's dreamscape. Every time Raj unfurls the white towel, fully holding it end-to-end with both his arms open wide, the towel becomes a reflector, a surface that throws sheets of warm light on his chiselled back, like a varnished, flexed landscape getting illuminated.

In his previous film, *Black*, too, there is a moment when you see how light changes the texture of an image by almost acting indisciplined, imposing its presence forcefully. Debraj Sahai (Amitabh Bachchan) is alone with young Michelle McNally (Ayesha Kapur), trying to teach her words, tame her wildness through meaning. She bites him. He screams, a shriek that rings at the very second there is a power cut. We see all the lights in the bungalow snuff out—his scream made that much more pungent by this sudden loss of light; the loss of light made that much clearer by his scream. Michelle's mother comes with a candle. We see its reflection on the wax-polished surfaces as she floats through the corridor. She enters the room with Debraj and Michelle. The camera, slipping into her shoes, glides towards Debraj and as the camera gets closer, a soft pouch of light from another world leaks on him. It is only then that the candle comes into frame—though it is clear, rationally speaking, no candle emits a light so soft over a patch so vast.

It is at such moments that you realize that it is light, under the baroque hands of cinematographer Ravi K. Chandran, which flushes an image *to* life. If we have taken light's presence, its god-like veil of visibility, for granted, then Bhansali notates its fire through the images he concocts with his cinematographers. As if saying, here, see light, and through light, my cinema.

I ask again, then. How do we consume a dream, this half-formed, full-throated world?

Saawariya is the one time that Bhansali has managed to show an entire city from a height, the very first shot of the film. But it isn't actually an image as much as it is a painting of a city, tinted blue, seen from a height, Buddha in the foreground and the bulbed turret of a mosque. Below is a city of bridges, waterways, Turkish domes, British roofs, and a big, creamy moon.

When people, rather simplistically, say that Bhansali's frames are like a painting, they mean that they possess an attention to detail, as though he is literally carving and chiselling every inch of the frame into existence through conscious, studied labour and intuitive, slippery artistry.

Paintings are not only seen but read and luxuriated over with one's aching attention. I want to borrow what artist Areez Katki, who works primarily with textile and their embedded histories, said in a walkthrough of his works, that embroidery is like slow drawing, to spin the idea that painting is like slow photography, and to thus call attention to the painting-ness of a photographed image, is to call attention to the slowness, the pedantic, arthritic labour, and languorous time that made it possible.

Here, however, he actually used a painting, a CGI train smoking across this city. He had no intention of realism, perfectly fine with artifice, perfectly confident that this artifice wouldn't translate into doubt or distance. That these are worlds—worlds we know don't exist—we will still yearn for, not as mimetic exercises, but as acts of submission.

In pursuit of beauty and perfection, of the gentle thrust, the poetic gestures, had he forsaken what too many consider the very foundation of a film—its story? As though Bhansali, on the precipice of a strong career, was waiting to take a sharp, downward exhale.

I ask again here, can we conceive of a criticism that privileges beauty over narrative; that conceives of emotion over logic, not as though they are opposing ideas, but ideas given different, disproportionate care.

The only slit from which the outside world enters this city of dreams is cinema—a screening of *Mughal-e-Azam* at the waterfront; sex workers singing 'Ae Malik Tere Bande Hum' from V. Shantaram's *Do Ankhen Barah Haath* (1957), like a prayer; *The Gold Rush* (1925) being screened at the theatres in *Black*; posters of *Nirala* (1950) outside Roshan Talkies in the beginning and, towards the end, banners of *Jahazi Lootera* (1957) in *Gangubai Kathiawadi*.

But while in *Gangubai Kathiawadi* and *Black*, cinema is marking time—letting us know that we are in the 1920s or early 1950s or late 1950s—in *Saawariya*, cinema feels like it has been imported from the land of time itself.

The old women are singing songs of *Mughal-e-Azam* as though they have watched it for decades, hundreds if not thousands of times. Where could they have watched it? There are no theatres, no television, save for the screen they put up at the waterfront. Cinema, too, like most cultural references, was osmotically, selectively sapped into *this* world.

World-building is an expectation as much as it is an excuse. On filmmakers, it imposes a demand for coherence, to create strands that can be tied back to the world in which the movie is being seen; to not take a leap so egregious that the thread snaps entirely, floating away. For spectators, for critics, it is an excuse to dismiss a world as much as it is an explanation for why they bought into that very world.

What does this demand say about the way we interact with cinema, or art, generally?

Slow dissolve.

The origin myth of cinema, an urban folklore. Paris, 1896.

The Lumière brothers are showing their fifty-second documentary film, *L'Arrivée d'un train en gare de La Ciotat*, or *Arrival of A Train at La Ciotat*. The camera is on the platform, askew, facing the train as it chugs onto the platform. As the train is approaching on-screen, in the audience, a murmur of anxious sweat sweeps through, a dark mortal fear crippling them, wondering if the train would leap out of the screen and crash onto them, pixels deposing into matter. There is panic in the theatre.

Over the years, we seem to have inured ourselves from this awe, simply because our minds have gotten used to it, made peace with the make-believe darkness. This fear, however, gave way to a strange kind of devotion—towards the gods we see as heroes, like *Jai Santoshi Maa* (1975), a low-budget mythological tale that shattered box office records, with people removing their slippers before entering the theatre, showering the screen with coins, flowers, and rice as though they were partaking in a ritual; or the heroes we see as gods.

Cinema's attempt to colonize all possibilities of storytelling had begun—to shoot things defying gravity, defying time, defying the imagination, even. The French essayist Paul Valery, in the 1960s noted, 'profound changes are impending in the ancient craft of the Beautiful'. From what I see, this reliance on technology has begun to confuse scale for sweep. Awe is increasingly being mistaken for beauty.

Which is why, when we call something, anything, beautiful, we must reconsider what we mean by beauty, if we mean anything at all.

While awe comes from the technical enterprise of a film, and keeps us at a distance, appreciating the labour, the innovation, the genius, beauty pulls us into the cinema itself, and it is *this* beauty that we have lost the capacity to feel our way through and pulsate with, what theological lecturer Jessica Frazier calls 'our vast imaginations [pulled] in the opposite direction from our small, frail bodies.'[8]

This is a fragile distinction, between awe and beauty, one even Bhansali is unable to make as he moves into historicals as his preferred genre, giving us sweeping visuals of wars and forts, as VFX begins to dominate his image-making, taking over it, sometimes drowning it.

But we still have a few years, a few films to go before that. With *Saawariya*, he was still battling the very idea of world-building.

While his cinema was attempting to eviscerate our sense of self, on the other hand, through cinema, we were craving to deepen our sense of self, invoke our logic, the limitations of our world, our experiences, our sensuality, our imagination. To see world-building as a logical demand, is to, thus, imagine cinema as a way of affirming the self. It is a strangely narrow, but perfectly acceptable, and a rather oatmeal posture.

For Bhansali, however, world-building is a peripheral concern. His fixation on beauty is so total, his faith in its power to demolish any demand—for coherence in world or character or plot, in visuals or narrative or time—consummate. The world is built. The way you would never ask a god to explain his creation, the way you would not be expected to explain the world that you rummage through like breath on an everyday basis, he refuses to have his world explained. He might fling a line or two to sate your agitations, to state the film's egregious pose of irrealism. But there is no desire in his cinema to see your world reflected in it. It isn't mimetic. But that does not mean it isn't inviting. It just means we have to reconsider the ways we enter a movie.

The late Rishi Kapoor, a man not known to mince his words, had written about this film in his memoir, *Khullam Khulla*, 'When we saw [*Saawariya*] for the first time, I was aghast. I immediately recalled my father's film, *Chhalia*, which was Manmohan Desai's first film. It didn't run for even two shows. That story could never be made into a film. If only Bhansali had told me, I would have dissuaded him. *Saawariya* had Salman Khan, in *Chhalia* it was Pran sa'ab. Bhansali had Ranbir, Manmohan Desai had Raj Kapoor. Here it was Sonam, there it was Nutan. *Saawariya* had great music, so did *Chhalia*. *Chhalia* was set in the context of Indo-Pak relations. *Saawariya* had, I don't know how to describe it, a spaced-out blue or green background. People uncharitably called it a 'blue film'. Neither film worked commercially.'[9]

Take this most comical, frustrating criticism of *Saawariya*, that it is too blue, too dark. It is the kind of criticism that comes from a deep desensitization towards the pressure colour exerts on our senses, our being.

Colour can produce what Goethe calls a 'violence' upon our mind, a feeling of being violated, stimulated, suffocated, satiated. It is why children's clothes, in this day and age, are in pastels, to not 'stimulate' them too much, those eyes which are just opening up to a world, its shapes, its sounds, its scents, its colours.

When the anthropologist Anand Pandian walked through Carlos Cruz-Diez's installation Chromosaturation—three small rooms, each glowing fluorescent with green, then red, then blue—he had a distinct visceral shiver as each hue poured over him, 'I remember the slight twinge of nausea that I felt in the green room, the sense of being pressed upon by heat from above in red, and the involuntary sigh of relief that escaped me as I stepped into the soft blue of the final room.'[10]

The Soviet film director and film theorist Sergei Eisenstein, in *On Colour*, thought colour was 'capable of profound psychological revelation'[11], that to stare into the abyss of colour, was to feel unmoored enough to feel vulnerable, for something dormant or non-existent to be exhumed.

The painter Mark Rothko, who from the 1950s, till his death in 1970, only painted fields of hazy, full-bodied colour, stacked on top of each other, thought this complete lack of narrative in painting allowed for 'the elimination of all obstacles between the painter and the idea, and between the idea and the observer.'[12] It was radical. It was gorgeous. It was wasteful. Millions of dollars were spent in acquiring what millions of people thought was childish, unremarkable flinging of paint over canvas. And yet, when people stood in front of Rothkos—imposing as they are—they wept. The American art curator Sarah Urist Green boils it down to three things: monumentality; simplicity; stillness. Looking at his paintings, divorced from the world, from memory, from silhouettes, from meaning, something primal erupts.

Like when looking at the shadow of vapours when boiling water for your morning coffee.

Like looking at a glass window on a train, sunlight streaming through days, weeks, months of grime collecting at the edges, filtering the yellow.

The blues of *Saawariya*, a reference to Krishna's blueness, Saawariya being another name for him, produce this aching alienation, this feeling of being rootless but not restless. The shades are more dusk than dawn, the pall of an eternal night, an arctic winter. It closes the world in, without it feeling claustrophobic, sealing it without it feeling shut in.

Bhansali's idea of beauty, though, has a specific texture that he bred and flowered in studios—what he calls his temple, where he refuses to even see wires, cables, trash dangling around—and not in the natural world at large.

Take director and photographer Achal Mishra's latest and third feature film, *Ri* (2023), set in Ladakh. It is not a film to be watched as much as blue vapour to be snorted. There is nothing holding the film together except a singular conviction in the sublime and blue-drenched twilight of the mountains.

By sublime, I mean a very specific kind of experience, one that is distinct from mere beauty. The sublime is that which strikes the fear of god in you; that beauty of which you are afraid. Say, a towering, rugged brown mountain in the distance, pressed up against a blue sky, slowly darkening into night, one shaft of light from the clouds firing up a patch on the peak, a patch that slowly recedes as the shaft thins into darkness, and the day collapses. And so begins *Ri*, a film shot entirely in the twilight moments in the mountains, when day kisses night, when blue kisses black.

Edmund Burke in his treatise treats the sublime as something horrifying from which we get pleasure, like looking at the deep sea from the shore, afraid of its lightless depth, its vast oblivion, where though we are safe, we are feeling a kind of 'astonishment . . . that state of the soul, in which all its motions are suspended, with some degree of horror.'

Bhansali's cinema, by abdicating the natural world, has abdicated this sublime. It can *never* be that. Perhaps, it has no interest, inclination in being that. But even later, in films like *Bajirao Mastani*, when he frames scenes by the river, out in the open, exposed to the elements, he is unable to invoke the sublime.

His beauty, instead, is a chromatic experiment.

The ancient Greeks did not have words for specific colours, but for how these colours interacted with light, with the texture on which they existed. Their chromatic experience took all of it together, refusing to, like Newton, extract it into its individual elements, stratify it, and then label that. When Homer called the seas 'wine-like', he did not mean the burgundy colour but that the seas produced the same shiny impression of wine inside a cup. What the Greeks understood, what the scientists had no interest in, was the subjective experience of colour as embedded in the world, not an objective study of it as captured in a neat vial.

To call *Saawariya* blue, then, is to flatten its many, many shades into a pigment. The way blue, perfumed into life by the streetlamp, becomes black as we hit the penumbra is a different blue than the ones painted on the walls of the house in the day, hazy, milkier; the blue flower petals on Gulab-ji's terrace; the blue of her glassy earrings. They are all blue, but so differently so, they almost jostle uneasily under the same label. Sometimes, I feel, words perform a violence on our erotic, sensual imagination.

When, in the early twentieth century, Technicolor—the American company, also the name of their technology—was trying to convince filmmakers to use their innovation, flushing in sneezes of saturation into the black and white frames, they used the language of 'realism'. The argument used was that colour was indispensable to cinematic realism, 'to portray life and nature as it really is', as described by a colour consultant in a cinema trade journal in 1935.

But realism was not what it was used for. Ironically, it was the opposite—flights of fantasy in musicals and

Westerns—that colour was used. In India, it was used for dance sequences in otherwise black and white films—*Kanavane Kankanda Deivam* (1955), 'Jab Pyaar Kiya Toh Darna Kya' in *Mughal-e-Azam* (1960). It is this legacy of using colour to express the bizarre, the outrageous, the delusional, that Bhansali, through the blueness of *Saawariya*, is somewhat tapping into.

But then, when colour becomes mundane and indispensable, directors and cinematographers begin to think of it like air—something that just happens to be there.

Pandian citing artist and critic David Batchelor's coinage of 'chromophobia', notes how modernity, particularly in the West, considers raw colour as 'feminine, vulgar, and primitive by nature' and tries to tame it with the help of technology. When these foreign platforms and studios leak into India, their expectations, too, throb our art. The colours in our films these days do not seem to have this embodied presence, floating pixels; there is saturation but no vigour, no vitality. In the time of Netflix's metallic realism—where all their images are colour corrected with the same, firm hand of sharp tints—how to think of image-making? Are we even thinking of 'image-making', obsessed as we are with 'storytelling'?

In short, can the image *be* the story?

Rishi Kapoor, though, was, in a sense, right. The story of *Saawariya* is a little too thin, vaporous. The whole film hinges on the question of whether or not the lover will return. A painful, yet moving portrait of unrequited love, the story itself isn't propulsive and is uninterested in the deeper psychology of its characters. Instead, Bhansali crowds the runtime with music—nine songs, roughly four minutes each, in the course of his two-hour film, which together pool to around a third of the run-time. The songs still the narrative, even as they massage its possibilities, extending an idea, a feeling emerging from the story—love, playfulness, joy, festivities, pain. Drawn to stories 'establishing' things, grounding them firmly—narrative, intent, character—songs are, instead, spaces where things float and fabulate. It is the movie taking an *angdai*, an arms-stretching, back-cracking yawn.

Saawariya offers an extraordinary glimpse of what Bhansali can do with music, and of his strong tether to the legacy of Hindi cinema, those simmering songs from films of the 1940–50s where directors filmed entire song sequences as close-ups of their actors wincing, being coy, being flirty, being hurt.

Just the face, and what luminous faces, capable of holding your attention, your desires. Think of the songs of Kamal Amrohi's first film *Mahal* (1949), with 'Mushkil Hai Bahut Mushkil', an almost-four-minute song, shot in one take, fixated entirely on Madhubala's spectral visage; or the way the camera catches the small, brusque flexes of flirtation on the face of Waheeda Rehman in 'Jaane Kya Tune Kahi' from *Pyaasa* (1957); or the pathetic sadness on the face of Meena Kumari in 'Na Jao Saiyan Chhuda Ke Baiyan' from *Saheb, Biwi, Aur Ghulam* (1962).

This requires an alternate way of thinking about cinema, where, according to Lesley Stern and George Kouvaros, 'the focus is on the way energy is deployed and transmitted by and through the body rather than privileging psychological or mimetic principles'.[13] Usha

Iyer is at the forefront of this theorizing with respect to Hindi cinema, where she looks at the 'binarization of the categories of acting and dancing', at shifting the focus from 'realist, speech-driven emoting' and taking more seriously 'performance that is not located only in the face—the most celebrated expressive field for evaluating 'good acting'—but across the body in dancing legs, gesturing fingers, gyrating torsos, emoting necks and heads.'[14] While Iyer's shifting of the gaze involves thinking of the labour that makes these songs possible, I am more moved by the mere presence of these bodies annexing space to express a feeling—not develop it, not merely state it, but to, through the body, warp and weft around it, thickening its being, if not its depth. The theatrics of being, the beauty of it, the flaring fabrics of 'Yoon Shabnami', the serene sea of men in white, Ranbir Raj in velvet red. And the dance itself, the spinning of the self on the axis of the body.

Think of Deepika Padukone in 'Mohe Rang Do Laal' from *Bajirao Mastani*, where she dances as Radha, and has to mimic her wrists being twisted by Krishna, the bangles on them, too, have to be broken, mimicked, and together, they have to produce both the pleasure of watching her dance and the abrasiveness of the gesture, which itself is never shown.

The first time Ranbir Raj (Ranbir Kapoor) lays eyes on Sakina (Sonam Kapoor), the movie ruptures into music, 'Masha Allah'. He walks with her, saves her from a drunkard, and with her on a boat, him steering it, docks as the song comes to an end. The entire song is an exchange of glances, with the grace-struck body flung around—the way she leaves her shawl behind, the way she runs along the banks. You can almost hear the question foaming, forming in the mind of the maker. When the body is so present, so sensually stirred, why bother with what steers them, their interiority?

Violence in Beauty, Violence as Beauty in *Ram-Leela*

Bistar yeh tera mera, arre jang ka maidan hai.

Oh, this bed of ours, it is a battlefield

—Siddharth-Garima

Have you ever experienced sex, pleasurable sex, as violence?

There is a spiky, moving video on one of the many X (formerly Twitter) accounts that unabashedly parade videos of pornography, among other things—the sex they have had or seen; the intimacy, raw and performed, that they exhibit; their nudity, dangling genitalia, aroused or resting. The video is from the Folsom Street Fair 2022 in San Francisco, an annual congregation of the Bondage, Dominance, Sadism, and Masochism (BDSM) and leather subculture. Among the many, varied aspects of BDSM is the consensual inflicting of pain and humiliation upon the person you are having sex with, or upon yourself, pain as pleasure, indignity as desire.

There are two men in the video. One of them—the submissive, sub as they say—is completely naked, his jockstrap pooled around his ankles, his hands above his head, crossed at the wrist. His elbows are resting against one of the trees by the streetside. The other man—the dominant, dom as they say—wearing only a jockstrap and harness slaps the sub's ass, flogs him, the butt cheeks quaking like chilled jelly. The dom turns the sub around, who was until then looking away from him. They kiss. A crowd is forming around this couple; others are walking past them, paying them little or no heed. There is some more flogging. You can see the expression of pain on the sub's face. You can also see his erection. At one point, the dom comes up to the sub, kisses him softly and rubs the running tears off the sub's wet cheeks.

The crowd applauds. They kiss deeper. There is a cut, and we see the sub in the arms of the dom holding him tight, his fingers resting gracefully on the dom's bulging biceps, weeping. The Twitter account captioned this video, 'Beautiful flogging at folsom street fair 2022'.

Beautiful flogging. Beautiful. I fixated on how an adjective can cartwheel a noun into outer space. Beautiful. Can violence be beautiful? Is it, merely, a matter of consent, then?

That can't be it, surely. Beauty is intuitive; consent is constructed. How, then, can violence be flecked by beauty? If violence, by definition, involves some kind of violation on the self, and if beauty is, by definition, an unselfing, what is violent beauty?

Bhansali's cinema offers a strange pathway into this question, because in his films, the 'self' is not an embodied presence, it is perfumed. They are untouched by the politics of representation.

Known for the emotional violence of his plotting, what often goes unremarked is how Bhansali's characters carry physical wounds as evidence, emotional violence given a more festering, tactile, physical, literal shape—Nandini slashing her wrists in *Hum Dil De Chuke Sanam* out of heartbreak; Devdas whacking Paro's forehead with her own necklace right before her wedding to another man in *Devdas*; the brawl that Ranbir Raj gets into leaving his face crimson and wounded in *Saawariya*; Sofia's abusive husband whacking her with a bouquet of white flowers in *Guzaarish*.

These scenes, the way they are conceived, staged and framed, speak a language more convoluted than we are comfortable with. For one, they don't exactly condemn the violence, or at least they refuse to make what is morally ugly look aesthetically blemished.

To see blood rush from slits on Nandini's wrist as her arm arcs through the pool of water, its rippling evident in the webbed, turquoise reflection it casts over the room, is to see self-mutilation as an act of grace. The blood that pours from Paro's forehead, which Devdas smears with his palm as a ritualized act of marriage, filling the parting of her hair with marital crimson, is seen as an offering of oneself to marriage, of possession. Paro weeps, not out of any sense of being violated, but the realization that all she can carry of Devdas into her married life—with another man—is *this* wound. To, then, see petal blossoms unpluck themselves from their stems as they are smacked against

Sofia's marble skin, scattering in white rain, is to see violence as an eruption of beauty.

There is an uneasy relationship we have with his ambivalent treatment of such moments, like the uneasiness we might feel watching women in a horde jump into a flame as a final, elegant act of rebellion in *Padmaavat*. Their beauty, their baroque, blinding brilliance is seen as something staged over the corpse of modern feminism, of a warped understanding of consent, of dignity.

A psychoanalytic impulse kicks in. You must be wondering, what would prompt a man to refuse to see violence against women as a violation on-screen?

There is a shaky, though not entirely dismissible, assumption here. That producing violence on-screen, as artists, is driven by an impulse to produce violence off-screen, a spark that cannot be sated in real life, and so is given sanction through the imagination, using fiction as a coping mechanism, a veil. That our response, as spectators, to violence on-screen is, somehow, emblematic, of our response to violence off-screen. Complicating this, Sheldon Pollock clarifies in his essay, *The Social Aesthetic and Sanskrit Literary Theory*, 'rasa refers to the reader's emotive response to literature and especially the uniqueness of this response, the fact that we take pleasure in sad stories, for example, but not in real sadness.'

In this view of art, whatever we produce, artistically, is somehow a manifestation of our inner demons, our very being. That the imagination is a mere shape given by our biases, our beliefs, our limitations—political and aesthetic. This is a very narrow conception of our confounding inner world.

It refuses to see the aesthetic as a realm of pure fabulation, untouched by or indifferent to the political and aesthetic pressures of reality. Despite Bhansali invoking his childhood, his mother, his father, while discussing his work—conspicuously absent in all this wallowing is the figure of the lover—Bhansali feels, to me, what poet T.S. Eliot called a 'mature' artist, impersonal, whose life sublimates into the style with which he expresses his inner world. As Eliot writes of the mature poet, 'Impressions and experiences which are important for the man may take no place in the poetry, and those which become important in the poetry may play quite a negligible part in the man, the personality.' [1]

Besides, there is no doubt that the foregrounding of ethical demands has made art a more predictable, palatable drone. You can see in criticism today the insistence on 'themes', what a film, a work of art is 'about', what are the moral distillations that are relevant, etc. The texture of thought desecrates the texture of sensual engagement. Cinema is being read like a manifesto. Cinema is being read.

Few will, for example, tell you that the director Shyam Benegal was responsible for bringing some of the hottest actors of the 1970s together, on-screen—Naseeruddin Shah, Girish Karnad and their porn-staches in *Nishant*, Amrish Puri's oiled muscularity, Shabana Azmi and Smita Patil exuding what can only be terribly described as dusky sex. It is true that themes of caste segregation, feminist politics, rural landscaping, and general subaltern representation pulsate in these early movies, which served as a roadmap for a certain kind of aware, and locally brewed cinema. But this discussion has always happened at a distance from the surface of the film, as though the surface—the very thing which draws us into that world—is an inadequate, frivolous space to fixate. As though its beauty somehow undermines its political significance.

It is because beauty is viscerally intuitive, but politics is cerebrally constructed, it is because beauty is shaded by our biases, and politics is the hurdling over of these biases; it is because politics allows us to be more aware of ourselves, less slippery, more certain. It is this fetishization of certainty, of clarity that has produced a strangely inert style of virtuous criticism.

What would be the kind of criticism, then, the kind of viewing that is a return to the surface?

By thinking and reducing our experience of art to its 'about', we have gone deeper, perhaps, but also in the words of art critic Sean Tatol, 'negate[d] art itself in favor of generic sentiments . . . a way of seeing that reduces art to a resolved formula'. [2] More than resolved, I suppose, this framework thinks of art as resolvable—the capacity to shape-shift a square peg of amoebic art into the round hole of moral certainty. Where art is final, declared, unamenable, this kind of critique hopes for a malleable dialectic. It is hopeful but, perhaps, naive. To keep art eternally unresolved.

What is also true, however, is that the violation of women on-screen has a testy history. On the one hand filmmakers have been accused of exploitation-filmmaking showing the act of grotesque violence with atomic detail and lush patience, making the violence feel visceral, overstating it to the point of making its beastly pleasures vicarious.

On the other hand, filmmakers like Bhansali have been accused of completely ignoring the violence that props up his vision of the world as a beautiful studio. Violence, not as vicarious or voyeuristic, but as vaudeville valium.

With *Ram-Leela*, this tendency erupts again, more frequently, more violently, more troublingly, guns blazing, rapes, loot, the physical body has now begun to stand in for the soul, its blemishing, the lashings it receives, all literal.

Ram-Leela is Bhansali's reimagining of Shakespeare's *Romeo and Juliet*, grafted onto a reimagined rural Gujarat. Following the sombre blues and greys of his preceding two films—*Saawariya* and *Guzaarish*—here is a chromatic rampage let loose. Reds bleed, as blood, as chilli, as red turmeric, as alta, as gulaal.

Ram (Ranveer Singh) from the *Rajadi* clan falls in love with Leela (Deepika Padukone) from the *Saneda* clan. The Rajadis and Sanedas have been historically at war for 500 years, we are told, the kind of war that is essential to cement identity. Outside of their war, they have nothing that divides them. To hold onto their respective identities, in order to hold onto pride, their *ghuroor*—Bhansali's favourite word, woven into dialogue, from *Devdas* to *Ram-Leela* to *Bajirao Mastani* to *Gangubai Kathiawadi*, beginning with *ghain*, the Urdu alphabet pronounced with a guttural 'g' followed by a hollow 'h', like clearing your throat—they must keep this war fuelled. Violence, in this film, edifies one's place in the world.

But first, lust.

Ram and Leela meet at a Holi party in the Saneda mansion. Ram and his entourage slip through without any Saneda person's knowing. When he first lays eyes on Leela it is the kind of playful attraction that is immediate, throbbing (read: horny), but also something that, like darshan, stains you.

He has a fistful of gulaal. She slaps it away. He sulks. She panders; comes to him with a fistful of gulaal—as reparation, as offering, as play. With him still sulking, she stains the ends of the fingers of her other hand and rubs the gulaal on her cheek, her neck—look at how Padukone's fingers flow as she moves her fingers, like water, fluid, a boneless grace that runs past the ridge between cheek and neck. He is interested, aroused, her hand, as a surrogate for his. Ram mimes, with red gulaal, that she should apply it on the parting of her hair—as a symbol of marriage, their marriage—before slipping his hands to his lips, rubbing it with lascivious intent. The muscles on her face rearrange from joy to doubt, even anger, obstinacy or *akkad*, as they say. She flings the red gulaal in the air, creating in the midst of all that chaos, their own sealed cauldron of desire, a barrier but also a force field of intimacy, and kisses him, the red on his lips, now on hers. He is dazed. She winks—to the beat, this is a Bhansali creation. Then, they dance, socialized and sputtering in circles, until the Saneda men are made alert, and he is chased out of the mansion.

One of the many mythological stories that underpin Holi, celebrating the love of Radha and Krishna, is of an anxious Krishna, dark-skinned, wondering if fair Radha loves him. His mother pushes him to ask Radha to apply colour on him, which Radha does, staining his face and validating his love, their love. If the application of gulaal on the face of the lover is a gesture of love returned—in 'Tum Tak' from *Raanjhanaa*, 'Haule Haule' in *Rab Ne Bana Di Jodi*, and 'Tere Rang' in *Atrangi Re*—Bhansali, in 'Lahu Munh Lag Gaya' turns this gesture into foreplay, blurring the demands of love and lust.

That the story of Radha–Krishna sees fairness bestow affection on darkness, that the divine dark-skinned lover is seeking, in both insecurity and anticipation, a response, is given a fragile interpretation in Bhansali's cinema, where the actresses are always a few shades lighter, given the politics of desirability in commercial Hindi cinema, inflected by both patriarchy and racism; fragile, because the one seeking validation is not always the darker one. Later, for example, in 'Mohe Rang Do Laal' from *Bajirao Mastani*, Mastani (Deepika Padukone) wearing all white, dances in front of her lover Bajirao (Ranveer Singh) with gulaal in her hands, points to her parting, looking at Bajirao and demanding to stain that split red. In *Padmaavat's* 'Holi (Manganiyars & Langa's folk song)' Padmavati (Deepika Padukone) jousts with Ratan Singh (Shahid Kapoor), flinging gulaal at his Rimple and Harpreet Narula couture, touching his feet, inviting him into the room as he rubs her with colour.

Both 'Mohe Rang Do Laal' and 'Holi', despite celebrating Holi, are largely monochromatic songs. In the former the reds of the hand and the lining of her *choli* puncture the white; in the latter pink powder clouds the golden. This is Bhansali jousting with conventions, as he has been doing throughout his filmography—to utilize the many shades of one colour, and to celebrate that range as he would celebrate the range across a spectrum. It is often hard to notice these rips given how blinding the predictable beauty of his movies can be. But they do exist, his frisking with tropes, a rest of rigidities.

Bhansali uses this seething animosity between the Rajadi and Saneda clans to build a bridge between lovers;

anger getting refined into desire. Every time Ram and Leela cross paths, their gazes don't meet but fight—'*nazar ladh rahi thi*,' she says when they speak for the first time. Expressions of desire quickly evaporate into fumes of anger which swiftly precipitate as lust again.

Take the scene where Ram is in Leela's bed. They have just met. They speak as though they have known each other for years. It is strange, their love. Before they have even spoken, they kiss. She asks for his number, he gives her his card, she tucks it into her blouse, he lustily reaches out to retrieve it.

She slaps him away, 'Aye!'

He roars back, 'AYE!'

Her fire burns, 'AYE!'

A soft silence.

He leaks out of anger into charm, caressing her face, 'aye'

She relents, smiles, 'aye'

Their lips come closer, as he mutters, 'aye'

She lets out a soft breath, 'aye'

Her hair gets entangled in his beard as he softly kisses her ears.

That the itches of anger and affection can be so close to each other is not new to Bhansali's conception of love. When Devdas smacks Paro on the head, making her forehead bleed, it opens up a language of love as violence in his cinema. That you would only violate those you love. Punish them with your absence. It's a brutal worldview, like emotional, not just physical, bondage.

These scenes are made palatable by the sheer, brazen fact that the women are never afraid of their men. Even when Ram rips his voice at Leela, her gaze never wavers.

When Devdas whacks Paro, her eyes don't flare from the shock of being battered. Threat never looms over their bodies and the way they crumple. When they do crumple, it is only out of grief, loss.

It is an odd image of the strong woman that Bhansali is creating—to be beaten down, but never intimidated by this violence. From his first film where Manisha Koirala played the shackled daughter to parents who are speech and hearing-impaired, to *Padmaavat* and *Gangubai Kathiawadi*, where Deepika Padukone and Alia Bhatt play the titular character, respectively—a privilege mostly reserved for heroes—Bhansali has always placed his female character in this gauzy, complicated limelight. There is such a thing as a 'Bhansali heroine', always confined by circumstances, and yet asserting herself, such that even her victimhood is framed like victory. His characters, especially the women, all emotional descendants of Meena Kumari or Guru Dutt—per his description—inhabit a fractured beauty that he milks to the hilt. Usually, it is love that tests their being.

With *Ram-Leela*, however, Bhansali was wading expressly into the waters of lust, a world where Ram heaves to his friends, '*Pant mein kaleja che*,' his heart is in his pants. Here, Bhansali dissolves the boundaries between love and lust, that distinction making no sense in this movie where initial eros, like paint, dries up immediately as longing, and it is the intoxicating fumes of this romantic sex—though their love is never consummated, something coming in the way of their sex—that draws one to another, that collides the fate of two lovers from warring clans.

While violence in love can be neatly filed into sutured categories of morality, violence in lust is a little more complicated. There is a penetrative violence in sex, which is part of its very character—pain and pleasure cuddling side-by-side in the murky waters. It is why the slapping around, jostling, wrestling for space, for power, even playfully, does not feel as morally conflicting as that in, say, *Devdas*. To be slapped in bed requires a very different kind of negotiation than being slapped elsewhere, clothed.

Breaking into the balls-to-the-wall song 'Ishqyaun Dhishqyaun' when they are courting each other in the early hours of the film, Ram and Leela kiss the opposite edges of the barrel of a gun. They slap each other in jest. She faux elbows him. He faux punches her. She faux kicks his balls. He spanks her. With each act of playful violence, Leela's tight bun gets looser and looser till her hair comes completely undone when he pushes her against a wall. When they dance, the gesture is that of a hand mimicking a gun thrusting in the direction of their loins.

The jest and jostle are embedded in each other, with his chiselled chest bursting from his barely buttoned shirt, and her waistline and cleavage that he keeps clinging onto. He pushes her to the ground and pulls her leg as she keeps bouncing on her hands. Her lehenga, deep indigo blue, embedded with sequins, keeps glittering in the shifting movements, exposing different shards of the fabric to the light, like patches of a starry night sky. Entwined, they are rolling together in the fading moments of the song.

This is a more tenable idea—violence in lust as opposed to violence in love. That desire is incapable of being politically well-behaved. It is a heady impulse, not a studied response to the world.

But what of just violence—that pure venom, untainted by any tenderness?

Take the scene where, later in the film, Leela's sister-in-law Rasila (Richa Chadha) is assaulted in an act of revenge by Ram's clansmen. The strings of her choli untied by erotically charged men, her body hoisted up into the air, being touched and groped, the neon pinks and candy floss purple lighting of the room spitting their citric breath on her body. Or even the scene where, to venge this violence on Rasila, men from Leela's clan chase Ram's sister-in-law Kesar (Barkha Sengupta), the lota that unhinges from her hip, to slowly tumble down, water whipping out in slow-motion arcs, a peacock perched on a tree, serving as a spectator. What a strange softness of tone to express the hardness of a scene.

This is not the kind of filming that draws you into its frame to participate in its violence—the voyeuristic gaze—but invites you to pass your hands over the texture of this brutality, that is potently and painstakingly conceived so as to never look brutal.

And that is a discomforting part of what you see; that it never *feels* like violence, you never worry for the characters, you do not insist on their safety, there is no tensile string thrumming in your heart, hoping the violence stops, or is averted. Bhansali's violence is unviolent, the un-ness being the gift of his cinema's beauty, unselfing the characters from their bodies.

That is the thing about beauty, it can make you forget the very point of the thing it is inhabiting. It can make another point, a parallel point, a palimpsestic point, a more pungent point that tugs more emphatically at your attention.

It is, perhaps, why beauty is considered with reservation. Implicit in this reservation is a belief that beauty is blinding, crowding out the possibility of anything—virtuous politics, narrative continuity, ethical clarity. If there is beauty, there is *only* beauty. Think of all those times you were advised to keep your guardrails up, unyielding, and strong when dating a more beautiful person? There is this worry that in the company of beauty, you will have forgiven, forgotten, or failed to notice something sinister. The red flags, with which Bhansali drapes his characters.

This mistrust of beauty is not new. It has plagued us since the Greeks, made most explicit with Plato—that poetry, like art, and by extension beauty, have no tether connecting it to truth.

Generally speaking, to think righteously and to feel sensually are not mutually exclusive. But suddenly, here, we begin to see them as opposing forces. To hold onto your politics is to let go of your sensory impulse, to stem it strongly with your thoughts. What people are axing in their insistence on the political wretchedness of Bhansali's cinema, is their ability to submit, testing their lunge into the frame. It can sometimes feel like pinning flowers onto a wooden board to make sense of it, because to see the flowers in the garden, those heady scents would warp us, unsteadying the demands of our mind.

None of this is meant to encourage violence against women. It is to say that Bhansali's cinema belongs to the tradition of the garden, not the board, it refuses even the slightest expectation of rightness, righteousness, because all his characters are stewing in desire and desire, like beauty, has the power to 'un-self', to do things, feel things that do not align with the image of ourself.

There is a question here that lingers, and this is about Bhansali's capabilities as a director. Does he not know how to stage violence as anything but beautiful? Flipping the question 'Is beauty the only thing he craves?' to 'Is beauty the *only* thing he can frame?'.

Here, I offer a counter. There is a cruel scene in the film where Leela's mother, the don Dhankor (Supriya Pathak), to punish her, hacks off her ring finger—which still has the ring Ram gave her—with the brass nut cutter. It is brutal, the violence so textured and osmotic, you turn away from the image, you crumple into a foetal position, because the way the body has reacted, the way most bodies would react, is to imagine this violence inflicted on the self. The opposite of beauty, a grotesque selfing, Bhansali is capable of invoking this, too—look at the cut of the nutcracker singeing into the skin, the sound, the aftermath stitched into one switcheroo of violence. He chooses not to evoke this in scenes of sexual violence, of assault.

As he chooses not to in, say, *Padmaavat*, when he wants to show the slaughter of an animal as sacrifice, before Raja Ratan Singh (Shahid Kapoor) goes to war. We see him wield the sword, slashing it downwards. We don't see the animal being dismembered, but we hear the 'khach' sound of the slaughter, and a necklace of blood that falls into the water, alchemizing violence into elegance.

Even in the pivotal scene in the early hours of *Ram-Leela*—the one that sets the film's conflict rolling—where Ram's brother and Leela's brother, in a drunken game, shoot bullets at each other's beer glasses, is suffocating with tension, a worry throbbing the scene, that the bullet will now hit flesh, not glass. It finally does. Ram's brother collapses in blood. As instinct, in grief, Ram pulls the trigger on Leela's brother.

So Bhansali chooses to deploy tension and aversion when he considers it necessary for the scene, and, perhaps, the assault on women is not considered worthy of that. It is lacquered by beauty, instead, part of the clan's barter of violence with violence, a mundane trade.

After killing Leela's brother in this brawl, Ram comes to both apologize to and run away with Leela. They escape. Ram's friends find out where he is, give the address to Leela's family who yank her away, back home, in a pre-interval scene that is not only one of Bhansali's most pulping—with both lovers screaming each other's names from a distance—but also, his most visually open scene; it was shot not on a set, but along Lake Pichola in Udaipur, Rajasthan.

It is here that we see quick zooms, a hand-held roughness, a quick gliding of the camera, horizontally, vertically, in the camera of cinematographer Ravi Varma—things we considered anathema in Bhansali's image-making. Remember, Ravi K. Chandran, the cinematographer he worked with before on *Black* and *Saawariya*, noted in an interview with critic Baradwaj Rangan, 'Hand-held camera and everything . . . he will get thrown off.'[3] And here we are, with those bawdy shakes and winking thrusts of the lens.

Ram-Leela marks a new kind of visual language in Bhansali's filmography. With every cinematographer, Bhansali's image-making gets a makeover. If Anil Mehta gave his visuals a more instinctive, incidental beauty—as though they emerged without labouring towards it—in films like *Khamoshi* and *Hum Dil De Chuke Sanam*, Binod Pradhan grounds that beauty with more calculated, symmetric, and thoughtful compositions in *Devdas*, one that would be taken increasingly seriously with Chandran's lubricated chiaroscuro in *Black* and *Saawariya* and Sudeep Chatterjee's neatness in films like *Guzaarish*, and later, a perfected, creamy shadow-lessness in *Bajirao Mastani*,

Padmaavat, and *Gangubai Kathiawadi.* With Chatterjee, the texture of the actors' skins began to look unusually smoother, like porcelain.

With *Ram-Leela*, it felt like Bhansali was becoming more playful, or was at least allowing that playfulness to emerge to the surface of the film more forcefully. Ravi Varman made the blur as dramatic scene transitions (where in *Black*, it was also used, though it felt more like a fade out, given the colour scheme), his characters emerging out of or dispersing into bright, glassy shards of light; elsewhere, the flush of gulaal is used as a scene transition (where in *Hum Dil De Chuke Sanam*, it was also used, though the tinsel of the lantern was not as apparent as the gulaal) there are strong back lights that turn the edges of a silhouette into a mirage, a shimmering heat; hard zooms were used in Ram's introductory song 'Tattad Tattad' as comic bursts, and in this pre-interval scene, as something bringing visual dynamism to an emotionally volcanic juncture in the story. It felt like Bhansali was letting go, even if it was within the narrow guardrails of his pursuit for beauty.

Varman used Rembrandt paintings as a reference while colour correcting, that same rush of colour to patches of skin, of colour applied as texture. In some sense, Rembrandt is a great launching pad. This seventeenth century Dutch artist was, in the words of art critic Sebastian Smee, a threat to classical values, of 'nature idealized, decorum upheld, vulgarity disdained'[4]. This film is a hatchet to all three. Nature is pulverized here, with peacocks killed and sent as vengeful gifts. Then, think of the song 'Tattad Tattad' with boxers peeking out through the denim, the *kediyo* untied on a sculpted body. Ram's video parlour is called 'Sweet Land'—land to be read as *lund*, or dick. Vulgarity is the language of affection, and decorum has been shelved, with two rambunctious characters, too big for their family, too big for their history, but big enough to *create* history.

This zig-zagging movement of the camera in the pre-interval scene I had not seen before in his filmography, nor anything like it—Leela is being pulled ahead by her brother across a crowded market, the camera is ahead of them, looking up, smoothly gliding backwards, and as Leela unhooks herself from her brother's grip running back, the camera, too, moves, trailing her, changing direction, moving forward; but then her brother reaches out, grips her hand harder and flings her to the ground in front of him, and the camera zaps backwards, smoothly. A movement that feels improvized. So much of this scene is shot with the camera looking up, framing trees and whitewashed buildings as backgrounds against which the characters howl and harangue. (This posture of the camera looking up would be used increasingly by Sudeep Chatterjee, to invoke the feeling of sitting in the first row of a theatre.) When Ram, trying to reach out to Leela, jumps into the lake, the water splashes back, and a few drops fall on the frame, blurring into bokeh as the sunlight glistens.

From this point, however, *Ram-Leela* feels a little unstable in its telling, because, often, it isn't clear whose intentions are known, and whose aren't. Leela is made to believe that Ram was the one who told her family of their location, humiliating her and her clan.

Does she believe this?

Can she not escape again?

Why does he not fight for her, find her again?

Instead, he becomes the leader of his clan, and visits her secretly at night, watching her from the window, to see that she is safe, sleeping well. When her finger is chopped as punishment, he chops his, too, inflicting on himself the same violence that was inflicted on her—if he could not protect her, then he must punish himself.

What are these compulsions that the character holds onto? This is a little like Devdas writing a letter to Paro—after his father gives him a dressing down when he finds them together in each other's arms at night—telling her to forget their love, only to return on the day of her marriage to someone else, to apologize for writing that letter, taking his words back. What compelled him to write that letter in the first place?

It is the family that looms large over these characters' sudden, unspeakable self-depredations—their worries, class anxieties, etc. But while *Devdas* spends time establishing the hold of the family over the character's imagination, *Ram-Leela* spent its entire first hour expressing how both Ram and Leela are standing at a slant to their ancestral demands, indifferent to the traditions of enmity that they have inherited. And yet, they boomeranged back to it, becoming its custodians. This sudden, jerking motion plagues the film.

The above questions, inadequately dealt with, are however rendered irrelevant, hammered into oblivion by the sheer emotional force of the film's drama. Truth is not something the film, his films, generally, are in search of—emotional truth, rational truth, narrative truth—because truth requires equanimity, and because his cinematic language is one of both abundance and scarcity, of too much being expressed, and not enough being said. This too muchness and too littleness nestling side by side is what Mexican essayist Carlos Fuentes calls 'baroque'—another definition of a word I have used and defined differently before—'the language of those peoples who, ignorant of the truth, look for it eagerly'[5]; that Bhansali does not know, instead, he finds.

This is something Bhansali has an unusual mastery over. His characters often act and react in ways that are questionable, even uncharacteristic, and yet, this never throws a shadow over the film, because the film's dramatic thrust and blinding beauty is so strong, it bulldozes narrative doubt.

In one of the most emotionally serrated scenes from Bhansali's filmography—the other being *Devdas'* climax—Ram and Leela meet as respective leaders of their clans, discussing trade, so there can be peace between the two groups. She enters from a blur, becoming a silhouette, and then lit by the harsh light entering from the windows. There is a deadness in her eyes. She is more formally dressed, as is he. All that eros and glistening skin has leaked out; his chest is covered by his buttoned black shirt, her hips and cleavage folded into her buttoned blouse.

She needles him into dust. When they list out their balance sheet of despair, their litany of disrepair, her accusing his family of killing her brother, him accusing hers of killing his brother, her accusing his clan of violence against their women, and him repeating that accusation back, saying his wife was taken away from him. Here, she rips, leaning forward, one foot on a higher platform, asking if he chose to avenge the loss of his brother, the assault of his women, why did he never avenge the loss of his wife—of her, though she refers to herself as an abstract other, 'biwi', as though her past were someone else?

This question, like thick dust suspended mid-air, was what was lingering throughout the second hour of the film, in our heads. It is here that we realize that this question was merely expected to be asked, not answered, for there is no answer.

Ram is silent.

Bhansali, especially in his later years, post *Saawariya*, is in the business of stylizing questions, propping them with poise and pulp, unable, unwilling to provide any emotionally neat response to any of it. His earlier films, *Khamoshi* and *Hum Dil De Chuke Sanam* were, relatively speaking, more resolved. *Ram-Leela* is his messiest film, because it deals with emotional ambiguities, refusing to iron them out even as it acknowledges them.

Ram, then, in one of the most moving literary uses of sublimation, distils his identity into that of his clan. When Leela proclaims that tobacco can be his domain, and '*asli* smuggling' be hers, Ram weeps, '*Aaj se saara nasha hamara, hosh inke havale*', that from this day on, the intoxication is ours, and our sense of self with them; when she says that they will give his clan neither bullets, food, nor brides, he laments, '*aaj se na hum goli chalayenge, na khaana khayenge, na shaadi karenge*', that from today, he will neither shoot bullets, nor eat food, nor marry, the 'hum' in his reply referring to both himself and his clan, in a stunning narrative crumbling of self. When he becomes his clan, himself becoming themself, how will he ever bridge the gap, that chasm, with her?

This exchange, charged with regret but not resentment, is what he calls '*khule aam pyaar*', love out in the open, sealing it with a manifesto, '*Dushmani nibhayenge, pyaar se*', that we will pursue our enmity, with love.

What is this love?

What is this enmity?

It is as if these words begin to lose their meaning the way it is fraying through the film. It is the film's frustration that it cannot express itself except as a contradiction, a complication. It is to the film's credit that none of it matters, burying itself in eros first, then yearning—neither needing more context than the sparse flings of dialogue given. Just as they found each other, suddenly, they lose each other, suddenly.

It is not just physical, interpersonal violence, but with *Ram-Leela*, Bhansali began thinking of large crowds bulging in blood. The clumsy climactic Dussehra spectacle, would, in his later period films—*Bajirao Mastani* in the eighteenth century and *Padmaavat* in the thirteenth century—refine itself, with both these latter films chock-full of war sequences, transforming the battlefield into a theatre to exhibit Bhansali's wares, stained by his love for flaring fabrics, choreographed chaos, and loose, long hair.

When my mother, watching the trailer of *Bajirao Mastani*, fixating on the image of Mastani (Deepika Padukone), the warrior princess on a horse, with war regalia and a helmet over her hair, untied and fluttering, asked me, 'Why can't she tie her hair, she is going to war?' I had nothing logical to say.

It is true that war would require women to tie their hair into neat buns, so it doesn't get caught in nets and knives. It would make it easier to fight, the strands not getting in the way of her vision, her violence.

And yet, what a silly thing to expect.

And yet, it is here, in these blood-blooming battlefields, where Bhansali's vision cripples.

He doesn't stage war as much as choreograph it, the *dandpatta* becoming not a weapon in combat as much a prop in the dance of metal. War requires scale that cannot be concocted on a set. It requires a more tranquillizing vision—one that can soften the hard contrasts, understand the demands of VFX, and is able to temper it into the world of the movie, not impose it.

The skies in Bhansali's war sequences have this greasy sheen, the heat looks dirty. His forests are plasticine. The greys are like puddle water. The oranges look tainted. The blues look muddied. While both *Bajirao Mastani* and *Padmaavat* have some of Bhansali's most stunning, delicate imagery—like Mastani (Deepika Padukone) wearing all white in 'Mohe Rang Do Laal', dancing with gulaal in her hands, pinching her lehenga to move her feet, but the touch is so delicate, the red of her hands doesn't stain the white; like Khilji running into a sandstorm caused by the chaos of war—they also have some of the most repugnant frames from his filmography.

Bajirao (Ranveer Singh), a Maratha peshwa, battles alongside Mastani, a Muslim warrior princess, falls in love with her and takes her as his second wife, turning his first wife Kashibai (Priyanka Chopra) to a maudlin mess, and causing his family and the larger Brahmin entourage to oppose every step of this inter-religious union.

The power and poetry of Bajirao and Mastani's last breath—they died as they lived, together—is shattered by the grotesque, grimy colours, the apparent visual effects of horses treading on water, Bajirao's hallucinations, the sky looking like lead. Even the searing climax of *Padmaavat*, of women howling into the fire as varying shades of red, is completely undone by the fire itself, so grisly and un-fire-like, it twists the very essence of a scene, yanking you out of it. If beauty has the power to 'unself' oneself, ugliness 'selves' that much more profoundly. You are suddenly aware of your aesthetic limits which are being transgressed so uncharitably.

It isn't like Bhansali knows exactly *what* he wants, but he knows exactly what he wants *to feel* and reverse engineers the materiality of his world. His briefs to his team are often bizarre. Cinematographer Sudeep Chatterjee told Film Companion that decoding Bhansali's vision is like playing a game of treasure hunt, where he keeps dropping hints and feelers, till you fling your art at his intuitions, and suddenly, something cracks. While deciding on the colour of Kashibai's room in *Bajirao Mastani* he told Chatterjee, 'I want something that makes me want to take off my shoes and sit on the ground'. 'I'll never forget that brief,' says Chatterjee. They went with pine green, touched by the breath of teal.

Parallely, Chatterjee and Bhansali would shuffle through paintings of Gaganendranath Tagore. 'There's this painting called The Procession which me and Sanjay tripped on. It's so dramatic and yet so muted. That was one of the key references,' Chatterjee notes. This painting, The Procession or Pratima Visarjan, keeps emerging to the surface of Bhansali's climaxes, be it the procession of Ram-Leela, the sucide squad of Padmaavat, or even the celebratory lap of Gangubai Kathiawadi. The crowds turn faceless when magnetized by the presence of the protagonist, hoisted into the limelight of death or destiny. There is luminescence, there is joy, there is also an aftertaste of melancholy, of mourning. This is after all the last day of the Puja, when the idol will be immersed, the goddess bidding farewell until next year, and the protagonists bidding farewell until forever.

For the 'Binte Dil' song in *Padmaavat*, he ordered Ranveer Singh to channel a mix of Zeenat Aman and Jim Morrison. What does that even mean? 'He has an ability to raise the stakes of the conflict while shooting a scene, such that achieving that golden standard feels like a moving target. He makes you feel like hitting that target is a matter of life and death,' explains Singh.

Then, what happened here, with these war sequences?

I think of the evening when the lawyer of Ethan Mascarenhas (Hrithik Roshan) in *Guzaarish* calls Ethan's doctor, worrying, having just heard of his desire for euthanasia, speaking against a dusk sky that looks ominous. Then, to see the evenings in *Bajirao Mastani* during which the battles are fought, a mousy grey mixed with saffron, the concoction of a machine that does not know how to channel a prompt into purpose, is to feel like a filmography lost at sea.

That he knows beauty when he sees it. But when he has to fabricate it on a computer, his impulses fray. When speaking to people close to the films about this chink in his armoury, I often hear of resource crunches, with lack of investment in both time and manpower to craft these images. Technology, an aide, is increasingly being used as though it was a solution.

My heart sinks every time I see the opening credits of *Bajirao Mastani*, a tiresome animated montage of the history of the Maratha empire, its wars and victories. There is a log of wood catching fire rolling down a hill, all animated, looking unlike wood, unlike fire. There was once an elegant dignity in his opening credits—the red of *Devdas* and *Ram-Leela*, the blue of *Saawariya*, which got swept up in the latest tech desires.

The opening war sequence of *Bajirao Mastani* alone, a seven-minute sequence, had over 300 shots—a mix of outdoor shoots and indoor shoots. This was one of the most demanding and ambitious sequences NY VFXWAALA, a Mumbai-based VFX studio had undertaken. The war sequence, shot during the day, was made into a night sequence on the computer. From arrows to soldiers to even the fort—all of this was created on the computer. It shows.

These VFX-thick films, *Ram-Leela*, *Bajirao Mastani*, and *Padmaavat*, resuscitated the Bhansali image in the wider public—after the failure of *Saawariya* and *Guzaarish*—while also radically revising what that image was. Bhansali, who was until then telling stories, began to now tell legends, from which morals—romantic, religious, feminist—leak. In this grand gesture, that went counter to the very fulcral evanescence of beauty, he was aided by the voice-over.

Leaning on mathematics scholar Peli Grietzer's jotting on X (formerly Twitter), 'Texture is just really fast structure and structure is just really slow texture'[6], Bhansali's cinema was emerging from texture, into structure.

The voice-over, like the visual effects, has transformed Bhansali's filmography to a point where it poses an obstacle to the very thing he spent his career foregrounding. Now beauty wasn't enough. It felt like it was in service of something else, something greater.

In a weak sense, Bhansali's career as a film director began with this voice-over, the voice of Annie (Manisha Koirala) in *Khamoshi: The Musical* holding our hands, ushering us into our seats, and into this world of lower-middle class Goa by the sea. In *Black*, too, Michelle McNally (Rani Mukerji), the deaf, blind and mute character introduces us into her world as the voice of god tracing the contours of the film. Then, in *Saawariya*, Gulab-ji (Mukerji, again), the sex worker with a heart of gold, bookends the film with her narration, explaining her '*khwabon ka sheher*', lifting us into its dreamy ether, the story of a wandering Ranbir Raj who runs into a mysterious Sakina one night, on a bridge—she is waiting for her lover, Iman; he is waiting for her to return his love. It is Gulab-ji who also, in the end, draws us back out of the film as the story closes in bitter-sweet abandon, with Sakina leaving with Imaan, leaving Ranbir Raj happy that she found love, but unhappy that this love, she could never locate in him.

For all the narrative duties they perform, these are not narrators or *sutradhars*. These are characters explaining their worlds, briefly, acknowledging the gulf between the world on-screen and the world from which people flock to the theatre. These characters are embedded deeply in the story they are telling, a subjective breath of meaning.

In this context, perhaps, *Guzaarish* is one of the most forthright films of his career, unmoved by a desire to explain, to mythologize. It begins with a slit of light that widens, a thick curtain being drawn open by Sofia D'Souza (Aishwarya Rai Bachchan), to exhibit a gossamer, translucent curtain that signals daylight by allowing light to pierce through. Sofia is the nurse and caretaker of the quadriplegic Ethan Mascarenhas (Hrithik Roshan)—this gets established in the first scene, when she brushes his teeth, undresses him, bathes him, and washes his hair with a matronly, platonic ease. The dialogues, per Bhansali's style, drip in exposition—that Sofia has been his nurse for twelve years; that he was once a magician, who, through a horrific accident onstage became a quadriplegic; that he, through his radio show, radiates hope.

Over the course of the film, a lot of the incongruities of the film are ironed out—Ethan's house is actually crumbling, not artfully devastated; he is deep in debt, not drawing salary from his past glories. That these incongruities had to be ironed out is Bhansali conceding to reality. While money has always been there, floating about the narrative—*Devdas*, for example, is actually predicated on a class-based conflict that severs lovers—economic security has rarely been on his radar. First, the poverty of *Khamoshi*, with Manish Malhotra's flaring frocks. Then, the poverty of *Guzaarish*, with Sabyasachi gowns—the text and the paratext i.e. the noise and news around the text, never cohere, and it is in this dissonance that we can find Bhansali's reckless disregard for world-building. That poverty need only be expressed in words, not visuals. That you do not need to believe their poverty, merely acknowledge its space in the larger scheme. That the rich fabrics and glistening jewels of their material lives are not expressions of their stated poverty, but Bhansali's inability to let raucous, grand beauty go, even as he invokes poverty for dramatic thrust. Complicating this is the notion that beauty can only be incubated in large, grand spaces, that poverty, like asymmetry, is unamenable to beauty.

Towards the end of *Guzaarish*, when Ethan tries to convince the courts of his euthanasia petition, Bhansali secretes one of his most complicated climaxes, where, despite the courts rejecting the petition, Sofia promises him that she shall end his life with the dignity he desires. He proposes they marry. She says yes. The last image is of Ethan laughing, crying, with his wife and friends cuddled around him, singing the chorus of a Goan song. As director Vikramaditya Motwane, who assisted Bhansali on *Hum*

Dil De Chuke Sanam and *Devdas*, observed, 'He loves catharsis—smiles with tears, and tears with smiles.'

But how do you milk this complicated feeling into a satin bow of a voice-over? You don't. You end it as airy and ambiguous. How does Sofia euthanize Ethan? What of her life after? Jail time? It is irrelevant. One of those moments where Bhansali's strong hand as a filmmaker was present—that only this much is the story I want to tell, as knotted as it might feel.

The closest Bhansali comes to making use of the sutradhar, so to speak, is in his film following *Guzaarish*—*Ram-Leela*. The film begins with an outsider—like us—entering a fictional Gujarati village Ranjhaar, where guns are being bought and sold in the market, like vegetables. He is on the phone, expressing his shock—our shock—at such a world existing. When a gun is shot at a child, he is horrified, '*Bachche pe goli chala di?*' For the people in Ranjhaar, however, this is part of the texture of their days—bawdy, raucous, full of fire and riots, the literal and the symbolic.

That by the end of *Ram-Leela*, both Ram and Leela are dead—a shockingly inept image of them falling together after shooting each another—a death that transforms them from characters to icons. The last image of the film is a sea of people, dressed in mourning white, carrying the biers of Ram and Leela—in sharp, silken red—through a narrow gully as onlookers, including a peacock, watch from the balcony.

Taking his story and pinning it, like a butterfly against a board, something the sensual beauty of his films disallow, he milks his movie into a moral ode. A voice-over—one of the sarpanch—explains their death and the resolution that has come from it, '*Ab ghar nahin jalte, diye jalte hain. Diwali saath manti hai. Badla aur ghurror agar samandar ko banjar rann bana sakte hai toh aashiq iss banjar mitti mein bhi phool khila sakte hain*', it is not houses but lamps that are aflame, Diwali celebrated side by side, that revenge and pride can turn an ocean into a desert, and that lovers can even make flowers bloom in that desert. That love is not going to reverse the violence of revenge and pride, it is not going to turn the desert back into the ocean. But that it is going to sediment the bleakness with beauty.

There is a worry about legacy here, of how this love will be received by later generations, later centuries. This same worry is expressed in a voice-over ending *Bajirao Mastani* and *Padmaavat*, a female voice used in the latter—explaining the legacy of the respective stories, because it is extremely aware that love can serve as a cultural roadmap, by being radical, pushing past the stigmas of the day, the hurdles of the culture. It cauterizes his characters, anaesthetizing them, numbing them to their humanity, the worldly cross-currents in the midst of which they are elevated to myth.

I also sense a soft anxiety when films are explained like this, introduced and epilogued—these strangely formal, ornate, and sober epilogues began infecting his films, *Ram-Leela* onwards.

That the film, the world, needs to be set in context; that the film needs to lay down the tenets of its world, express its internal narrative and moral logic with clarity. I suppose it is an understandable urge, for Bhansali was coming out of two difficult flops—*Saawariya*, then *Guzaarish*—which produced a very loud consensus of criticism, which was primarily about the world, not the story. It felt too much, too obscure, too plastic, too set-like, too this, too that. It is kind of odd how so many are confident in expressing their inadequacy, in jubilantly celebrating the limits of their imagination, wondering why a filmmaker is not catering to their limits, their expectations of realism.

This is the central tension in film criticism, where we do not know where to locate the flaw—in the critic or the film? In the film's inability to grasp the critic, or the critic's inability to be grasped at? This tension is exemplified in the battlefield of Bhansali's cinema, because his style is so singular, so inimitable, so striking, it has this take-it-or-leave-it audacity stamped all over it. When people say they do not 'get' Bhansali, what they are confessing to is an inability to be swept into the world. A criticism actually sounds indistinguishable from a characterization of the film. Plot, characters, dialogue—these are mere formalities, filigrees.

That is also the problem with style that is so recognizable. When something is so apparent, it is easy to dismiss it, because it is easy to characterize it, and by characterizing it, easy to reduce it.

Even his writers are often blindsided by this full-throated extravagance. Bhavani Iyer was in her early twenties when she met Bhansali, when he took her on as his protégé, to write *Black*. Bhansali, fresh off *Devdas'* success, wanted to work with a younger writer, who came with her own burdens and oblivions, her own sense of beauty, her own life experiences to alchemize into narrative, and got Iyer's contact information from his then assistant Motwane. It was supposed to be a quick half-hour chat, and like most absorbing, meandering conversations, it stretched out over four hours. Iyer felt in sync. They wore the same colour. When someone placed a remote control on the table, they both reached out to straighten it. Iyer was not much of a cinephile, preferring the company of books.

She gave him book recommendations. He gave her film recommendations.

Even in this synced state, Iyer had no idea what Bhansali would do with the story she wrote, of Michelle McNally (Rani Mukerji), a deaf, blind, and mute protagonist, who finds the light with the help of her teacher Debraj Sahai (Amitabh Bachchan), only to come to his rescue when he descends into amnesia.

Michelle belongs to a colonial, aristocratic family. 'I had thought it would be in a bungalow in Colaba, not fully dilapidated but slightly worn out, you know. A street and some characters,' Iyer told Film Companion.

Then, imagine Iyer walking onto set, confronted by an imagination that ran so wild, so brassy, it flung her modest world-building into the dustpan.

She saw imposing buildings peppered with life-sized statues, 'When I write about an exterior beautiful cottage, I see a cottage. He sees a mansion. That is the difference between us. This was, probably, a very different way of interpreting the story that I had written, the narrative I had built. I surrendered to that.'

Iyer offers a more elegant, psychological explanation for this innate, intuitive grasp at extravagance, 'He likes to create something slightly larger than life. You know, not slightly, but a very larger-than-life world. It is almost like a world that he wants to escape into, to diminish the fact that, as a child, he didn't really grow up with a lot.'

When she broached this with Bhansali, he asked her if she had ever seen a chawl. Iyer, born and bred in Bengaluru, had never seen such poverty and its accompanying architecture. While driving back home that day, he showed her the chawls in Bhuleshwar that he grew up in. 'He even showed me his way of experiencing cinema. He would see it from a huge projection-screen on a white cloth where the image was projected. He wouldn't have the money to go to watch it in the theatre so he would see it from his house, which was behind the *parda* . . . I had to surrender to the way he saw or wanted to mount [his movies] because that for him is his expression of his demons, whatever he has, within him. When you have so much aesthetic within you, to be living in a house with a sewer running past you can be very troubling.'

There is something dainty here, which I must flag. We have this urge to explain a feeling, a filmography, to sort of perform therapy at a distance, diagnose a filmmaker's life to distil the origin story of their aesthetic.

For example, it is easy to see in Bhansali's depiction of women what Iyer calls 'the strong feminine influence in his life' of his mother, Leela Bhansali. 'She is strong, she is vulnerable, she is fun, she is tenacious, and she is feisty. She is everything. He has never seen women as *bichara*, someone to pity. He has never played that card with women.' To also see, in his depiction of ache, the unexpressed love he felt for his father, to whom he dedicates every film of his.

What this amounts to is a gorgeous, compelling myth-making of the man Bhansali. What it also does is strip away the mystery of being, by reducing every act of his into a determined culmination of his childhood. Reducing a life to a narrative by parading the subconscious as conscious, is also a kind of violence we inflict on it. What of the things he picked up along the way to complicate his relationship to women, to men, to the world? What of the inexplicable vagaries that our being consists of? The various hypocrisies his characters embody, which he finds alluring, even essential. In two of his films, *Devdas* and *Bajirao Mastani*, the central hero loves two women, and the women celebrate this shared love in dance through a homosocial embrace of their triangulating love, the Radha–Krishna–Rukmini framing; that they are both willing to let go, even if for a second, the possessive urge of love to celebrate a more abstract idea of feminine companionship? (And instantly forget that companionship. In both films, the scenes following their dancing have a strange silence around this companionship, as though the coming together never happened, as though it were dreamed up.)

To find in the film's surface a reflection of the filmmaker is as fraught an exercise as it is exciting. I indulge in it, the way I indulge in gossip—like cheap thrills, but careful to not mistake it for anything more than strands of possibilities. For that is all they offer—possibilities.

Besides, it is, perhaps, because the surface is this glistening and arresting—potholed and polished—that we expect an explanation. Like a voice within us saying, this is unusual, why does this exist?

There is also a wariness here. One that visual artist Mohd. Intiyaz expressed and clarified to me through his artwork. While exhibiting his wares at the Method Art Gallery in Kalaghoda, Mumbai, in August 2023, bunched together under a notorious title 'Baad Me Aana', a lot of his canvases—paintings of Muslim life in India, the social, the intimate—are hemmed in by these striking, arabesque borders in teal, red, green, and gold. There is embroidery, too, on the borders of the fabrics on display.

The association was immediate. These borders seemed to hark back to the Mughal miniatures, and their rich, thick borders of foliage, a dervishing swirl across centuries.

Intiyaz, however, is not convinced. In what I see as a continuing, cascading culture of beatification, he sees a facade. What are you beautifying? What are you shielding with your beautification?

On his way to Jamia Millia Islamia University, Delhi where he got his MFA in painting, he would always see people sleeping under the Nizamuddin flyover. Months later, after a vacation, when he was treading that same path, instead of the usual dusting of yawning people, there were, instead, flowers and trees, the walls were painted, with a board that said 'Beautification'. This displacement, this suspicion leaked into his work, along with patterns he had osmotically grasped from henna drying on hands, and from the artistry of his own family, who work in textiles.

It is this doubling that I find productive, tensile, and fascinating—to invoke beauty, and yet, to be suspicious of it. In trying to represent the Muslim life—figures are rendered translucent because their identities are slippery, many without paperwork; his mother praying; a man putting up a protest poster—he never renders it passive, and in framing the Muslim being in the cross-currents of these doubling pressures, he is doing with representation a slippery, meandering thing. He isn't allowing us to fixate on either the suspicion or the beauty, our mind, our senses tossing about, here and there, unsteadily.

Isn't this how we see Sofia D'Souza, the nurse and caretaker of the quadriplegic Ethan Mascarenhas, in *Guzaarish*? This same suspicion, this wonder about what she is overcompensating for. But that suspicion never stemming our ravenous grabbing at it?

Working for Ethan for over twelve years, she dresses in extravagant gowns and maxis, with jewellery dripping from her ears like golden drops, bright red lips. That she partakes in Bhansali's universe should foreclose any questions of realism—how can she afford this look? But there is a nagging question that trails the film. What is this beauty compensating for? It is the first time we are compelled to psychoanalyse a Bhansali character, because we are never allowed into her past.

That is, until one day, her husband comes and rips her off the face of the film—an abusive alcoholic. In an interview, Aishwarya Rai Bachchan notes, 'Through the course of the movie, as you learn her backstory, you realize that she's dressing up as much as she is hiding something.'[7]

Now, all of a sudden, her hand-embroidered handkerchiefs, her charcoal and cherry lipstick, her lantern sleeves, deep neck maxis, backless cholis, panelled skirts, coral *kanpashas*, rhodolite *balis*, butterfly earrings, minakari bird ring and the turquoise and coral ring—Sabyasachi debuted his jewellery line with the Navratan necklace that she wears in the climax—feel aligned. That these women douse themselves in shringaar because they are wretched.

If, in Bhansali's world, women need to suffer in order to be given dignity, is shringaar an overcompensating for the terrible life they are living?

The only reason we pay attention to these women, bruised as they are by circumstances thrown at them, is because they are beautiful. Beauty is not some embellishment. In Bhansali's cinema, it is perhaps the only reason these women exist. Beauty seems to be that which helps compensate for material realism with psychological realism.

There is this tension in Bhansali's films—of how much of the outside world to let inside.

In *Hum Dil De Chuke Sanam*, right after the interval, we see a car for the first time, an automobile that ferries people to and from places, and realize, this world of Bhansali is connected to the world. That Sameer, his protagonist did not have to rant and rave through a desert to get to the haveli.

Similarly, despite being set in this geographic netherworld, somewhere tucked in Gujarat, in *Ram-Leela* (2013), we hear of the cloudburst in Uttarakhand, of Ahmedabad—cities bustling and buried far away. The phone plays an important role. Lovers speak with phones glued to their ears, the villains conspire to kidnap over the phone, and the thirsting women excitedly photograph an oiled, bare-chested Ram (Ranveer Singh) using the phone's camera. The women, though, are dressed in traditional Gujarati outfits and prints, such are the pulls of tradition in the face of modernity.

The ringtone is a comic reprieve. Sexting is a thriving language of lovers. In many of Bhansali's previous films, he has often used the phone booth or letters as means of communication. The urgency of letters has been replaced by the immediacy of phones. The phone—a piece of technology that anachronistically places the film in the contemporary moment—is suddenly thrown into important scenes. After an intense exchange of words, Ram requests Leela for a photo, and gives instructions to his minions that this photo of the two of them must go on X (formerly Twitter) and then, the newspaper.

The thing about technology is that it signals flux. That information streams in, changing your relationship to the world through trickles of knowledge. But that is not at all what is happening here. This is Bhansali comfortable with the idea that his universe, a tender, torturously conceived universe, has its horizons, its limits, and thus, isn't endless. That it also has a sieved border through which other worlds leak in. That even as it doesn't have much of an impression on his world, a world beyond his world exists. It feels like defeat.

~

Another kind of violence was entering Bhansali's cinema with *Ram-Leela*—shorn of beauty, stormed by ugly rhetoric and frisking blood. This had to do with, perhaps, the civil society growing increasingly hot-headed and sensitive, with vigilante groups wielding a stronger grip over the popular imagination and public order.

Right before the release of *Ram-Leela*, the Prabhu Samaj Dharmik Ram Leela Committee, among six others, filed a petition at the Delhi High Court. That the film's name alludes to Ramlila, the traditional enactment of the Ramayana, the life and story of Rama, they were incensed. That the film contains sex, violence, and vulgarity, they and their religious sentiments were hurt.

From *Ramleela*, the film's name was changed to *Ram-Leela*, the hyphen insisting that the film is about two people, not one idea, and then, when even this did not sate the prudes, forty-eight hours before the release of the film, the name was changed, again, to *Goliyon Ki Rasleela Ram-Leela*, and Bhansali made a statement clarifying the film had nothing to do with Ramlila, and just that his protagonists were named Ram and Leela, Leela being an ode to his mother.

This violence also had to do with Bhansali's back-bending cinema, which looked at history as muse, squeezing his stories and their storied budgets from our past. Because as Bhansali took to history, history itself was becoming a contested ground, inflected by religious insecurity and political pressure.

While *Bajirao Mastani* had the historians baying for blood in newspaper columns—harmless, really—it is with *Padmaavat* that this blood manifested more literally.

This story—of a Khilji king's obsession with a Rajput princess—had been simmering in his radar for decades. In the 1980s, Bhansali had worked as an assistant editor on Shyam Benegal's *Bharat Ek Khoj's* episode titled, 'Delhi Sultanate, Part III, Padmavat & The Tughlak Dynasty.'

Then, after the humiliating failure of *Saawariya*, Bhansali retreated to Paris, where he was asked to direct *Padmavati*, an opera to be staged at the Théâtre du Châtelet. He did not know French, did not understand a word of Albert Roussel's score from the early twentieth century, and had never seen opera. He had to think of ways to force-fit the percussive rhythm of Indian dance to the smooth rhythms of the score, to bring theatrics to the opera, acting into singing. The New York Times, when they interviewed him, found it odd that he kept calling the singers 'actors'.[8]

Bhansali got a horse, an elephant, a young tiger, and even a python that had to be cancelled at the last moment, on stage. He received a fifteen-minute standing ovation. Though, not all were in rapture. The Guardian critic, unimpressed, called it 'a series of inert tableaux, to which some coarse acting and risible choreography adds nothing at all.'[9] (Beware of the biases that birth adjectives, lurking behind its safe cover.)

In 2016, he came back to the story, making this film at a budget of ₹215 crore, the most expensive Hindi movie at the time. In many ways, the movie departed from the opera. In the film, Alauddin kills Ratan Singh on the battlefield, in an act of deceit, further bolstering Alauddin's slimy ethics against Ratan Singh's iron-clad moral spine—which led to his downfall, the film almost working as a cautionary tale against such hard-shell beliefs of dull, unyielding respectability. Hearing of his death, his wife Padmavati, along with all the women in her entourage, drape themselves in fire. The film ends here.

In the opera, Ratan Singh—in the opera, it is actually Ratan Sen, not Singh—gets wounded in war and suggests to his wife that it might be best to surrender to prevent a massacre. Refusing this, she kills Ratan Singh and immolates herself on his funeral pyre. After this, the couple appear, ascending steps, as though entering the afterlife, together. Since the film was interested in exalting not just Padmavati, but also Ratan Singh as respective epitomes of Rajput feminine and masculine strides, Ratan Singh is martyred in the hands of his grimy enemy, the Khilji king, instead of mariticide, being stabbed by his own wife, surely an emasculating act.

During the making of the film, rumours brewed about there being a romantic dream sequence between Khilji and Padmavati. Anyone who is remotely familiar with Bhansali's filmography would know he sets his films in such stratospherically heightened and sealed worlds they have never needed a dream sequence or a dream song. But the rumour stuck.

In January 2017, at Jaipur's Jaigarh fort, members from the Karni Sena, a militant caste group, barged into the film sets and assaulted the staff, slapping Bhansali, who later agreed to delete the scenes he shot there. He made a statement clarifying that the film was made keeping Rajput pride in mind. Again, in March, the set was vandalized and set ablaze with petrol bombs, hurting animals and destroying costumes.

When the teaser came out in October of the same year, Karni Sena members vandalized a theatre where it was playing. They threatened to cut off Deepika Padukone's nose if the film released. There was a Rs 5 crore bounty on the heads of Bhansali and Padukone. The ruling party, BJP, decided to write to the Election Commission, Central Board of Film Certification (CBFC) and the Central government to hold the release of the film for allegedly hurting the sentiments of the Kshatriya community. This petition went to the Supreme Court, which rejected it.

As a concession, the film's title was changed from *Padmavati* to *Padmaavat*, turning a character into a myth, and Padukone's bare hips in a song were covered with CGI cloth. But when the film finally released in January 2018, it was at the receiving end of another kind of criticism—of glorifying immolation of women out of caste pride, a criticism we discussed in the introduction.

Nevertheless, the film became a blockbuster minting 585 crore, his most successful film, and Bhansali went radio silent. A year later, when he emerged to the surface, he told Film Companion, 'No filmmaker in the world has gone through or should ever go through [this trauma].'[10]

Other Kinds of Beauty in *Gangubai Kathiawadi*

Ye na thi hamari qismat ki visaal-e-yaar hota
Agar aur jiite rahte yahin intizar hota

It was not destined for the lover and I to merge
If I were to live longer, the wait for you would have been that much more . . .

—Begum Akhtar singing Mirza Ghalib's ghazal,
'Yeh Na Thi Hamari Qismat', which opens
Gangubai Kathiawadi

Let me begin with those uninterrupted, undammed, recklessly flowing sixty seconds in the song 'Dholida' from *Gangubai* Kathiawadi. One unbroken shot, these sixty seconds, a whirling, vertiginous trance, are perched at the end of the bittersweet celebratory Navratri song, more than halfway through the film.

Ganga Jagjeevandas Kathiawadi (Alia Bhatt), from Kathiawad, is trafficked by her boyfriend into a brothel in then-Bombay. We are in post-independent India. Over the years, through her beauty and wily, intimidating charisma, she becomes a '*kothewali*', the one who protects and promotes sex workers living under her, while not practicing sex work herself. She is rechristened Gangubai Kathiawadi, the steely, unshakable madam. But the stern, gruff strength she exudes is a careful performance.

Right before the song 'Dholida', there is a tremorous scene where she tries to reach out, via trunk call, to her mother whom she hasn't spoken to since she left home. She finds out, in the space of a dialogue patch, that her father, whom she doted on and who doted on her, passed away. The tone and words of her mother are ones of complete rejection. Apart from the keys to their almirah, all Gangubai has of her past life, the dregs of which she carries precociously, precautiously, poetically, is the garba, the cultural productions that we saw in the beginning of the film, where we are given a glimpse of her moneyed, luxurious life back in Gujarat.

The song begins with the visual of a lamp—like how 'Dola Re Dola' began, like how 'Pinga' began, all three songs of female companionship tied to festivals. The garba of 'Dholida' is both a celebration and a mourning—the dual tensions which Bhansali revels in. He is incapable of giving his characters the unsullied, unadulterated intensity of one emotion. Joy is always undercut by a simmering melancholy.

Think of when, in *Hum Dil De Chuke Sanam,* the celebratory 'Dhol Baje' is actually a memory, where Nandini (Aishwarya Rai Bachchan), unhappily married, is reminiscing in sadness, the joys of a life that she no longer lives.

Think of when, in *Guzaarish*, the joyful 'Udi' where the celebratory performance of Sofia (Aishwarya Rai Bachchan), the caretaker, to entertain Ethan (Hrithik Roshan), her paraplegic patient, ends with him weeping at his inability to move, to get up and dance with her, step for step.

That when two women who are in love with the same man dance together—in *Devdas*, in *Bajirao Mastani*—it is both a sakhi-dyed drenching, but also a revelling in the pathos of yearning, only half-fulfilled. When the tawaif Bibbojaan (Aditi Rao Hydari) dances with an erotic pull in *Heeramandi*'s 'Saiyan Hatto Jaao', it is the playful dangling of sex in front of her patron, but also, in her eyes, you see an unfulfilled yearning for something else—which the show soon clarifies; that she is a freedom fighter, infusing in erotic play a patriotic fervour.

The bittersweetness, then, of these final moments of 'Dholida' is not unusual. Neither is the length of the take. What is unusual is how Bhansali feels more comfortable renouncing total control over the protagonist, the actor. When Gangubai twirls, the sari—pearling white in a sea of earthen colours—swings clumsily. Its pleats are pinned as though they would never unpleat, rigidly folded, tied in the Gujarati style, from the front, and it dangles with this fragility. Cinematographer Sudeep Chatterjee's camera is facing up, from a hip-height, so you rarely get to see what the flares of the fabric look like near the ankles—no top shots, too, uninterested in the grammar of awe given the shamiana of fairy lights. When Gangubai reaches out towards plates of gulaal to smash into and fling a fistful into the air, there is a graceless grasping. We do not know which plates she will slump onto and which ones she will leave out. After her twirls, she is so disoriented, that when she reaches out for a plate, she is not even able to clench it. She falls into the crowd briefly. Her eyes are haywire in dizziness.

Later, in *Heeramandi*, Bhansali's first stab at longform storytelling, Fareedan (Sonakshi Sinha), a tawaif who, throwing tradition to the wayside, hosts a party for the suited-booted to which she wears a sari—as opposed to the *ghunghroo* and lehenga, or *anarkali*, or other such appropriate wear for the *mujra*. She dances on a table on which she was keeping her bare feet, flails her arms, flings her cigarette, and this sari, a ruffled sea of sequins, glitters under the light in soft waves as she moves about. Touched by a thrilling chaos, there is a sizzle in this song, of order and proportion and care being evacuated from the image. It almost deflates, a deflation that is, perhaps, the most fertile moment of the show, where beauty is the context, and chaos spins it elsewhere. Hands in the air, the underside of the sari—a creamy nothingness—comes into focus, and as she twirls around, the sari falls off, and it is held on merely by the pin on her shoulder. The underside of the garment, this is something that Bhansali takes care of, as well. When a lehenga swirls and the camera catches the inner skin of the cloth, what does it see? These, too, are discussions he has with his costume designers. Not because the underside will be seen, but it might, in the moment, become that which renders the song imperfect and troubled.

Beauty as proportion, as symmetry, as control, as awe, as produced by a ruler, a microscope, a reckless revision, a tireless number of takes—suddenly, all of this, which

Bhansali is known for, cease to matter. The climax of 'Dholida' are the sixty most unstable seconds of beauty in a Bhansali film, much like 'Tilasmi Baahein', refusing the 'screenshot', refusing to be 'like a painting'. This is not easy beauty. You cannot pause your way through it, it must be gulped as a whole

The instability of these sixty seconds is rooted in the idea of beauty we have received from the Greeks—Aristotle defining beauty as 'order and symmetry and definiteness', Plato expressing beauty as harmony that emerges from 'proportion', inseparable from 'truth'. The Enlightenment thinkers of Europe grabbed at the opportunity to bottle up beauty, and label it carefully, slotting it into their shelves—this bottle of silver bromide reads 'Golden Ratio', that bottle with pinecone breath reads 'Fibonacci Series', this naked little bottle reads 'Vitruvian Man', something that can be perfectly inscribed within both a square and a circle. Capturing it, like dyes in bottles, makes it possible to deploy it whenever, to control it. A pinch of the golden ratio, a dash of Fibonacci.

Bhansali's beauty, steeped in this tradition, suddenly, for those sixty seconds, looked away—not out of arrogance, but, perhaps, that, too. What I sensed was a desperation to forage other kinds of beauty, one that you can sense in the shifting light in the following paragraph, ripped from Chloe Cooper Jones's book *Easy Beauty*, 'Symmetry is predictable; I am soothed but not surprised. To say that beauty was merely a result of definite measurement deflated the mystery of the aesthetic experience: that bodily recognition, an ancient sense tuned to beauty, a physical seizing of beauty and of beauty's dissonance; a welcome fever, a palpitant thrill, pleasure ill at ease, a turned stomach, a chill, prickling hairs, goose bumps, high attention . . . I like the vastness. I want to keep the idea of beauty like a stone in my hand, turning it over and over.'

The turning over and over of beauty in the hands of Bhansali I felt here, after films where his preoccupation with beauty felt like it had reached its destination, spinning his stories with awe, instead. His sense of heaving immediacy, the hawk-eyed presence on the set, the improvizational, eternally unfinished style of his working can be seen here.

Bhansali even leached colour from his frames; there is a sepia wash that allows the metal work in Gangubai's white sari to cut through the image, for the lights in the background to feel more embedded, for the evening to look more melancholic, as though steeped in tea.

White is the predominant saturational force in this film. He has moved away from colour, to texture, to silhouette. He has moved away from tight, studied perfection to something more sandpapered and touched by the looseness of life.

It is true that white is a colour that occasionally punctures the riotous colourscape of Bhansali's films, like Mariamma (Helen) running into a field of nothingness with a white cloth in *Khamoshi: The Musical*, signifying her death, or the endless white cloth that is pulled from under Ethan's bed in *Guzaarish* as a parting gift of magic to his protege, or the white sari with a red border Nandini (Aishwarya Rai Bachchan) wears on her first night in *Hum Dil De Chuke Sanam,* or the fluttering white sari with a red border Paro (again, Aishwarya Rai Bachchan) wears in the climactic sweep of *Devdas,* or the white lehenga choli Leela (Deepika Padukone) wears to consummate her marriage, or what Priyanka Chopra

Jonas wears as the emotional surrogate of Ram (Ranveer Singh), enticing him while also expressing him. But white has never been the anchoring palette of the entire wardrobe. If anything, the whiteness of these moments was elevated by the sheer romp and splendour of colour around it. With *Gangubai Kathiawadi*, Bhansali was reconstructing his aesthetic.

From puncturing the riot of textures and colours, to being the only colour—that, too, is a choice that is both curious and radical. To have someone who has found beauty in the hues of the most pungent shades, to look back and say, perhaps, white is enough.

He even finds space in his narrative to give voice to this kind of beauty, when Gangubai waxes poetic about the different shades of white—the clouds, the salt, the froth, the moon, the paper, the rose, the snow, the milk, the conch shell—lost as she is in a reverie of pain and a life of ruin, one that the shadowlessness of white, somehow, softens.

With *Gangubai Kathiawadi*, Bhansali seems to have become more daring in his indiscretions. His love for beauty as that thing which holds your attention by its collar remains. But suddenly, he is gripped by a more adventurous spirit. Beauty is now embedded in the emotional core of a moment, like the impassioned, exorcizing tailspin of 'Dholida'. Beauty emanates from it, like fumes. It doesn't gild it. It doesn't frame it.

Another way I have been thinking about this slip, because it feels so tectonic, is that beauty has been used as the safe cushioning—the meticulous details of the set design, the costume design, the lighting—from which he leaps forth. Beauty is not that to which he goes, but that which allows him to get where he wants.

There is greater clarity as a spectator. When you are moved by the sixty seconds of trance, you are moved by its spinning, emotional cartwheeling, not blinded by its beauty, because the beauty here isn't blinding. The costumes don't invoke awe. The angles don't produce a sigh. The flaring of fabrics doesn't look like a coordinated attack on our blunted senses. To be moved by *Gangubai Kathiawadi* is a neater, less breathless dislodging of the heart.

Costume designer Sheetal Iqbal Sharma told me how, from the very beginning, he was aware that this Bhansali film is a sharp pivot in his filmography. 'He showed me a reference image—an old image from the '40s, of an old lady at the window wearing just a blouse and petticoat. It didn't look like an SLB costume—not the flamboyant Gulab-ji (Rani Mukerji) from *Saawariya*. Instead, he wanted to show the deeper, darker side.'[1]

One day, in the early days of conceiving the film, Bhansali asked Sharma to come to his office with an outfit of specific measurements—he did not mention for whom, nor other details. Sharma went with one outfit in English pastels, muted and serene. When he got to the office, he saw Alia Bhatt and her entourage and panicked. If he knew this was for her, he would have gotten more options, 'I had literally come with one outfit on a hanger. I aged it; it didn't even look fresh.'

That did not matter. Bhansali was moved by what he saw. So moved that he used it in the scene where, for the first time, Gangubai is calling out to customers. Bhansali even designed the entire doorway and the colour palette of that scene keeping that outfit in mind. That outfit, the same one which felt inadequate to Bhansali's imagination and Bhatt's stature at first, even made it to the first poster of the film.

This does not mean, however, that Bhansali's vision had watered down, becoming less demanding. Just that its demands had changed their posture.

Take the song 'Shikayat', a *qawwali* song, where the central erotic force—what I would have called an 'item' if I were a shady film producer, dick dangling—is a woman seated (Huma Qureshi). Throughout the song, she and her backup dancers are given a spot from which they don't budge. The choreography is built around this stasis. The beauty comes from the gestures—of plucking a segment of stringed jasmine from her hair and flinging it at the audience; of fingering her lace handkerchief from her blouse to fling that, too, at the audience. The stillness almost invites you to pay attention to the lyrics, the small exchange of eyes that say big, brutal things.

To be sure, there is drama, how could there not?—not just emotional and visual, but behind the scenes, too. Look at the glittering embroidery on Qureshi's sari. Sharma spoke of how the sharp sequins, the razored *zari*, and the intricate *zardozi* bruised Qureshi's hips and neck, and that in between takes concealer had to be applied to cover the bruises. Pain as beauty—pain as necessary for beauty. These are ideals that Bhansali's characters and actors both must endure.

Famous for his anger, for reducing most actresses to tears, for being flippant about 'method acting', but for being intensely demanding about the smallest details—like the *pallu* of a background dancer at the back or the dimming wick of one of the many thousand lamps in the background—Bhansali's cinema exudes a very specific, timely, kind of submission.

He does not care what you do behind the camera. He often speaks of how Rani Mukerji, while playing Michelle McNally, the deaf, blind, and mute character in *Black*, would be laughing and cheering with the crew, but when a shot was called, would snap into her character's muffled melancholy. He has dismissed Ranveer Singh's intense preparation, locking himself up to tap into some inner cove of darkness for his role of the rapacious Delhi Sultan Alauddin Khilji in *Padmaavat*.

Preparation is not something Bhansali marvels at. He prefers spontaneity, something emerging from a moment. Often actors would come to set with their lines learned, only to be given a fresh, new sheet of dialogues—dialogues often shot in long takes requiring both the emotional stamina to power through, and a memory to furnish that stamina. On the first day of *Ram-Leela*, when Deepika Padukone arrived with her lines prepared and was, instead, given a fresh sheet of long, winding, accented dialogue, she broke down. The entire choreography of Heeramandi's 'Tilasmi Bahein'—a song shot in one take—was changed on the day of the shoot.

What you perhaps see is a tempestuous man, impulsive—or, if you feel charitable, indecisive. But what if we shift the light a little and see what lurks in the shadow?

The idea that art is produced at a particular moment. That you can rehearse, prepare, workshop towards that moment, but it is the moment which is sacrosanct, above all else. If it does not feel right, it does not ring true, it should not be shot. Decisions and dialogues can be upturned. After days of shooting in a black lehenga, Bhansali decided that it wasn't working and re-shot a whole song—'Ang Laga De' song from *Ram-Leela*—in white instead, giving his designers a narrow window to fabricate and fabulate something new. The throwing of gulaal in 'Dholida', too, was a last-minute choice, sending Sharma's team into a tizzy, given the white sari and the red powder. Overnight, they stitched a sari, keeping six versions of that sari ready.

Bhansali does, however, take this idea of placing a moment above everything else—scheduling, mental health, budgets—to its logical snapping point, when he stops shooting for a day if someone wears an overpowering colour to the set, or if he sees wires dangling in tardy clumps.

Submission, often considered an act of romance, a wilful renunciation of agency—giving up the very thing that challenges destiny—with Bhansali, is woven into something both vital and violent; his movies and their making belong in that hazy corridor between madness and love. It is impossible to look away. It is impossible to not be disturbed.

Similar to 'Ram Chaahe Leela', 'Shikayat' too, had the dancer—the 'item girl', Priyanka Chopra Jonas there, Qureshi here—perform pathos as a mouthpiece, an emotional surrogate to express feelings the protagonist is unable to. There is a reason Qureshi is also wearing white in the song. There was a black sari, too, that was being discussed for her, but Bhansali insisted that Qureshi must feel and look like the alter ego of Gangubai, who is always dressed in white.

In 'Ram Chaahe Leela', the thrusts, the pirouettes, the acrobatics, are all overshadowed by a moment, when she decides, in a gesture of erotic coyness, to button up her blouse, instead of buttoning it down. This is Bhansali saying that eros has nothing to do with the depth of cleavage; that sex can be evoked from things other than nudity—like gestures, like winks, like the way you hold and sculpt space. The cleavage is etched in concealer, nonetheless. The point he makes here is not literal, and we would be fools to take him at face value.

I do not want to imply that *Gangubai Kathiawadi* is a complete, radical aesthetic pivot, but merely how some fixations of his have been dimmed here. Others—like the precision of a choreographed action to the beat of a song—remain. '*Sab kuch beat pe hona chahiye*', the beat is sacrosanct, he mumbles in a video of the making of a song.

Each string of a kite is pulsed, pulled, and released in the Makar Sankranti song in *Hum Dil De Chuke Sanam* to a rhythm. Even when, in the film, Nandini slashes her wrist during 'Tadap Tadap', the slashing happens when the beat pauses to swell up again, crooning 'Lut Gaye'. When Sonam Kapoor has to open a letter folded twice over in *Saawariya*, Bhansali instructs her to open it with a 1-2-3-4 rhythm in mind. When each card is flung into the air in 'Jab Saiyan' in *Gangubai Kathiawadi*, it is done to the beat. Each push, shove, invocation, invitation of 'Meri Jaan' happens to a nip in the voice, the body cresting with music, even if it isn't 'dance' in the choreographed, synchronized sense. The way Bibbojaan's body in Heeramandi tightens when she points her finger at her patron while dancing, only to slacken as the beat is struck, her fingers limp, as though the body inhabits time, space, *and* percussion.

In a whistling confrontation, Gangubai has just shown her political opponent, the hijra Raziabai (Vijay Raaz), her place by humiliating her. The next scene has to taper away from this throttling adrenaline. Cut. The camera glides gracefully as her friend Kamli (Indira Tiwari) runs through laundry lines with Gangubai's poster for the political campaign. Gangu is skipping on the terrace, the hem of her white sari dipping and dimpling with every thump of the skip, the pressure of the feet against concrete passing onto the fabrics, like electric currents. Kamli and Gangu chat, and Gangu invites Kamli to join her, and they skip together, the rope creating this bubble of intimacy, as they continue speaking, Kamli soothing Gangu's nerves about the upcoming election.

This is part of Bhansali's larger artistic thrust, which is to, through cinema, turn life into choreography, elevating even mundane acts to the lilt of rhythm—like eating biscuits, mixing sugar in tea in *Guzaarish*, of exercising, skipping in *Gangubai Kathiawadi*, of flicking cards in *Devdas* and *Gangubai Kathiawadi* and *Heeramandi*, of opening letters in *Saawariya*.

In *Gangubai Kathiawadi*, this desire to turn every interaction into a delicate dance is most profoundly realized. Sometimes, she is on the telephone, swinging on a *jhula*, when a man comes in with the film reels she asked for, and while she is completing her conversation on the phone with someone else, through gestures, she is having a parallel conversation with the man in front of her—kicking her footstool towards him so he can sit where her feet were to rest.

A student of Odissi, Bhansali understands grace as necessary to life, not as embellishment. It must seep into the very being, leak out of every pore. It is why the setting of this film, 1950–60s Mumbai, is a desperate recall to the last generation where grace was used, however romantically and myopically, to describe the gait of sex workers. The film doesn't touch the years of Indira Gandhi, ending shy of it—many considered the Emergency of 1975–77, with its erect-spine moralizing and forceful sterilizations, the beginning of the decline of red-light districts. It was also, as author Amit Chaudhuri writes, the era of the 'industrialisation of Lata's voice', industrialization being the loss of texture, Lata being the late Lata Mangeshkar, whose voice haunts Bhansali's imagination, despite never being used in his movies.[2]

Based on 'The Matriarch of Kamathipura', a chapter from S. Hussain Zaidi and Jane Borges' *Mafia Queens of Mumbai*, *Gangubai Kathiawadi* has an episodic rhythm to it, where people, like events, stain and flush out of the narrative, never to be seen again. Like his first film *Khamoshi*—also narrated by the female protagonist—leaps of time take place in *Gangubai Kathiawadi*, from her first night in the brothel to the anniversary of her first night, from her being beaten up to a month later, her demanding of justice. Time is embedded into the dialogues.

Love is merely one of these events. This, too, is an exciting choice. To mount a film on a woman's life, and to narrate the woman's story without love being the central conflict. Bhansali keeps playing up and playing down what is 'feminine' about her—a femininity he has nurtured and burnished since his first film, one that he undoes, completely, in this film. When the first teaser came out, with the image of Gangubai's feet on a chair, a beedi to her mouth, a colleague pointed out how it reminded her of Vijay from *Deewaar*—that same arrogance (or confidence), that same posture, that same determination, that blue.

We see Gangubai exercising—with weights, with a skipping rope, one masculine, one feminine—we see her steaming, we see her swinging, we see her cooking. She speaks like a man to men. She speaks like a woman to women. She speaks like a foe to a foe, a friend to a friend. She speaks like a mother to a lost girl; like a *shagird* to a saviour; like a matriarch to a cub.

The frames, from the very beginning, are packed with the feminine, even as the very ideal of the feminine is being shredded. Often, in scenes, you won't find a trace of men—either visually or narratively. In an industry where most films do not pass the Bechdel test—which looks at the proportion of dialogues in a film spoken by women, where they speak about things other than men—Bhansali's cinema has offered an idealized, brutalized feminine as the torchbearer. But this isn't a conscious, feminist posture as much as the inevitable climax of a worldview that prioritizes beauty and is able to locate this beauty only in the feminine. Naturally, the men blur out of focus.

There is also a consummate queerness with which she slithers through the demands of the world, queerness being what queer theorist David M. Halperin argues, 'whatever is at odds with the normal, the legitimate, the dominant'. It is more than an orientation of desire; it is an orientation of being. As José Esteban Muñoz writes, queerness is valuable, and of use, only in the horizon. And like most Bhansali films, the queerness in *Gangubai Kathiawadi*, of Gangubai staking her breath and butter at this horizon, is apparent seething *under* the surface.

At 'Queer Bollywood', an event organized by Ashoka University towards the autumnal glitch of 2022, Professor Madhavi Menon posed a question to the panellists—

professor and filmmaker Shohini Ghosh, critic Namrata Joshi, and me: Which film of 2022 was more 'queer', *Gangubai Kathiawadi* or *Badhaai Do*?

This question unsteadies. As a text, it is clear that *Badhaai Do* was queerer—with a gay and lesbian protagonist narratively arcing their way through the sentimental rigour of queer becoming.

And, yet, unanimously, we felt that it was *Gangubai Kathiawadi* which was more 'queer', because queerness traffics in something *more* than a sexual identity and the grasping of its emotional expression; it is far more expansive and elusive than an argument for dignity.

It is a thing in the air, a glimpse of the eye, a twitch of the hip, a biting of the lip, a graceful gait, a graceless confrontation, an exaggeration, an aberration; a perpetual, rose-tinted victimhood, of eternal longing, of eternal sex; of Begum Akhtar's voice beginning a film, of imagining yourself to be the protagonist of your life so insistently that you end up looking at the camera, breaking the fourth wall; of Huma Qureshi's white sari burdened by so much metal work that it kept bruising her while shooting, and of that concealer that needed to be applied between shots.

Gangubai Kathiawadi emerges into cinematic life with Begum Akhtar's voice crooning 'Yeh Na Thi Hamari Qismat'. That the voice of Begum Akhtar, once the courtesan Akhtari Bai Faizabadi, is being used to introduce the story of Gangubai, once a sex worker, is an important detail because it alludes to a slipperiness between the two, but also implies that an unfulfilled yearning connects both.

Ruth Vanita notes in *Dancing with the Nation: Courtesans in Bombay Cinema* that by the twentieth century, the distinction between a prostitute and a 'vaishya', a 'tawaif'—sexually independent women, courtesans, who would perform for their patrons and not necessarily sleep with them—had been blurred.[3] Mayank Austen Soofi, who wrote about Delhi's red-light district, GB Road, too, notes that over time, the sitar in the drawing room of these kothas would disappear, sold, to be replaced with disco lights as the decades aged post-independence.[4]

Akhtari Bai, the courtesan figure, would over time, through marriage to a respectable barrister, become Begum Akhtar. But even as she shed her courtesan past—and this was the time when All India Radio refused to have women who were not married sing on the airwaves—the queerness smudged hard.

In the 1960s, when she used to travel, she often used to be surrounded by two gay men—the poet Agha Shahid Ali and the historian Saleem Kidwai, both in their late teens, bewitched. Manan Kapoor, in his biography of Agha Shahid Ali writes about how Akhtari taught Shahid how to wield nakhra or affectations along with wit into a seamless performance.

When asked about being 'besotted' with her, the late Kidwai had said, '[E]very gay man I knew then, was in love with her music. I mean for gay men, her lyrics, which were mostly about heartbreak and longing, made a lot of sense. I don't know how it happens with this generation but in our generation, this was there. You fell in love with someone, and it might be a straight man who is not recognizing it or reciprocating it. Gay men knew all about the agony of being in love. It was the reason why Meena Kumari was so popular with gay men, too. She is suffering away, her heart is broken, and she's dying on a bed of tears. Drinking away her grief, both she and Akhtari.'[5]

Much like Akhtari, Meena Kumari—whom also Bhansali keeps referencing as an emotional Pole Star—according to Vikram Phukan, 'created a whole new sub-culture in the gay desi ghettos. Her mask-like face in the classic *Pakeezah* was a doppelgänger for the gay man as eternal victim, for Venus as a boy, for a kind of self-flagellating self-regard played out with baroque music and delicious melodrama. Even self-pity needs cultural trappings.'[6]

And why wouldn't the gay man be besotted by such grief, a fabulation of the self, as both gorgeous and grief-struck?

The word 'camp' is often flung around, though what it exactly means is a toss-up. Words, queerness has taught us, mean and matter only so much; what Derrida said about meaning escaping language. It is the conviction, the slanted wink with which they are uttered which matters. It is desire, like vapour, not the perfume but the perfum*ed*. Things *aren't* queer. They *feel* queer. Hence, *Gangubai Kathiawadi*.

It is in this context that I want to slice to the front what Professor Menon said, with respect to *Badhaai Do*: 'I suspect that all these films want to do is expand the ambit of the heterosexual, rather than outline a sphere of the queer.'[7]

That the film was expressly thinking about love *through* the prisms of marriage and child rearing as opposed to *Gangubai Kathiawadi* which stands apart from, looking askew at any of the institutions within which we are supposed to fit as we age. That even as Bhansali toys around with the aesthetic and narrative possibilities of heterosexuality, his cinema is expressly expanding the sphere of the queer, Bhansali's playpen, the litany of nakhras, a dictionary that expands with every film. That his characters often end up alone, dead, or grieving, speaks to a doomed destiny of queerness. That even as Gangubai ends up winning the love and support of her community, she is by herself, alone on that pedestal. That even as the women of *Heeramandi* have finally unified to fight the British, they are all alone, their lovers either forsaken or dead or merely inexistent.

Sometimes, however, queerness is made more conspicuous and undeniable, even if not in the full-throated vigour with which passion is usually expressed.

Actor Jim Sarbh describes Malik Kafur, his character in *Padmaavat* as 'Alauddin [Khilji]'s favourite wench'. Gifted to Khilji as a slave, Malik Kafur was both his confidante and concubine. The obvious sexual tension between the two—sitting at two ends of a bathtub, braiding hair, the lustful gaze, the arching of the back, and Kafur being called Khilji's 'begum'—agitated queer activists who were worried that Khilji's hinted but never explored bisexuality was framed as another of his barbaric vices. Historians, too, were squirming with a different kind of factual discomfort.

But neither concern seemed to be on Bhansali's mind, which runs on instinct, 'spontaneously reacting to the space' on the day of shoot. While Bhansali has bestowed upon his heroes a ravishing sexual energy—Salman Khan's bare-chested child-like charms in *Hum Dil De Chuke Sanam*, Ranbir Kapoor's marble butt serenading in *Saawariya*, Ranveer Singh's low-hanging dhoti revealing his Adonis Belt in *Ram-Leela,* the gym-stained, granite bodies of Tajdar (Taha Shah) and Cartwright (Jason Shah) in *Heeramandi*—these characters have rarely expended this energy on other men.

This was the first time he was dealing with homosexuality in his films, and he was not willing to be coy about it, even if he is not willing to verbalize it, merely expressing it through music, through glares stained with longing, unrequited but never dismissed. Later, in *Heeramandi*, when he would allow his characters to express their queerness with more clarity, their men bedding men, their women bedding women, it felt that much more disturbing, because he was unable to imagine queerness as inseparable from scheming, sleuthing villainy—delicious, scheming, sleuthing villainy, but scheming, sleuthing villainy, nonetheless. Ditto for the hijra politician Raziabai (Vijay Raaz) in *Gangubai Kathiawadi*. Their queerness came out along with their ill intentions, but so did their chomping, gluttonous joy. You can read homophobia into it as easily as you can discern villainous camp, the phobic and the joyous holding hands.

Bhansali's brief to Ranveer Singh on the day they were shooting 'Bint-e-dil', with Sarbh and Singh sharing a moment in the bathtub, was 'Jim Morrison, Zeenat Aman, mix the two.' There were no rehearsals.

The song is an elaboration of the desire, a pit fire of seduction, Malik Kafur feels for Alauddin, even as Kafur sings of Alauddin's lover, his *bint-e-dil*, the girl of his heart. The camera resorts to shooting them both from behind cloth surfaces, reducing them to threadbare mirages of themselves; it feels, almost, like voyeurism, or if you are prone to metaphors—why, though?—the emotional veiling that longing produces.

Sarbh notes how the palpable sexuality in the film is not studied, but spontaneous. In a scene, Khilji, throwing bird seeds around him, turns to Malik Kafur with his hands held out. Sarbh was directed to eat the bird seeds from his hands, looking embarrassed. But the scene wasn't working for Bhansali. He then turned to Sarbh and asked, 'What nautanki were you going to do? You were going to do something else at that moment, nah? Okay do, do, do.'

Sarbh went down 'blowjob style', neither embarrassed, nor demeaned. 'It doesn't embarrass me to eat from my king's hand. I don't give a fuck. That's the whole thought behind a submissive in a BDSM scenario,' Sarbh notes.

~

They sneak into hearts, and sometimes beds, selling false love, but always experiencing true pain. You can recognize them quite easily, because blaring disrepair is their badge of honour—'*dil mein aag, chehre mein gulaab*', heart on fire, but cheeks blushing—and they perform this pathos in every loud glance and attended gesture. If alive, they end up alone.

Bhansali's art keeps returning to these courtesans and sex workers—emotionally feral women, brothel madams, performance artists, vice-riddled mavens. It might seem at first like his preoccupation with these ravaged women is yoked to his preoccupation with beauty, grace, and eros. The courtesan and sex worker figure are, in Bhansali's cinema, the repository of these very virtues—shringaar, *adab*, and nakhra—without which he cannot imagine either his world or his women.

At first, it was Chandramukhi (Madhuri Dixit Nene) in *Devdas*. Then Gulab (Rani Mukerji) in *Saawariya*. Soon after, there was Mastani (Deepika Padukone) in *Bajirao Mastani*, Gangubai Kathiawadi in the eponymous film, and then, the clump of courtesans in *Heeramandi*—

Mallikajaan (Manisha Koirala) and her daughters Alamzeb (Sharmin Segal) and Bibbojaan (Aditi Rao Hydari); her younger sister Waheeda (Sanjeeda Sheikh); her elder sister Rehana and her daughter Fareedan (both, Sonakshi Sinha); adopted daughter Lajjo (Richa Chadha), among others. *Heeramandi* is, essentially, a war of adab between Mallikajaan and Fareedan, their claims clashing, their ploys tormenting, until through the sympathies of sisterhood—from, say, the rape of Mallikajaan for which Fareedan feels responsible—they join hands to thwart the British.

In Bhansali's world, we respect—or, at worst, sympathize with—these women only because they are able to alchemize their violations into a glittering, unforgettable performance, the kind that makes grief aspirational and all-consuming, the kind that makes character-building redundant. Their mere presence is enough to desecrate any conservative demands for the character's meandering path, their arc and their growth. Bhansali's characters flicker, they don't become. For instance, Lajjo's entrance into *Heeramandi* is her alcoholic longing for a nawab who never returns it; and her exit is her alcoholic, poisoned longing for a nawab who never returns it—between the two, she mewls, resplendent in imported georgette.

Must women suffer, then? Then, women must suffer.

Historically, a line separates the sex worker from the courtesan or 'tawaif', which comes from 'tauf', to move; or 'kothewali' or 'ganewali', referring to their place of work and their marketable skill; or 'veshya', which comes from the same root as 'vaishya', or merchant.

Distinctions, however, are often not made; the women are considered fungible figures. And when the line is drawn, it is made at the cost of the sex worker, in pursuit of some hazy, romanticized 'culture' that the tawaif promotes.

The tawaifs, the most educated of their time, were sexually and economically independent women. The kothewalis of Lucknow, for example, were the highest taxpayers and even owned property. Many even joined the revolt of 1857 as prominent revolutionaries—a revolutionary zeal Bhansali lends his tawaifs. There is something delicate here, though—that these tawaifs were propped up by a dense but fragile network of patrons, hinged on their voice, their *adaa*, as much as their body. They did enter into sexual relations with their patrons, though not exclusively; not always, and certainly not everyone.

Post 1857, in the wave of British vengeance, courtesans were affected as morality laws refused to see them as more than sex workers, as vectors of disease, their property being appropriated. It was not just the British, but also the reformers of the late nineteenth and early twentieth century, who not only kept their distance from the kotha culture, but actively condemned them. For example, when Gauhar Jaan, India's first recording megastar, was going to be present at an Indian National Congress session, this was objected to by the women. She raised money for the Congress, nonetheless. When Gandhi did not show up to one of her fundraisers, sending a representative instead, it is said that she donated only half of what she promised. Later, courtesans like Jaddan Bai helped fund the left-leaning Progressive Writers Association. They were essential even as they were fading.

The muck, though, stuck. As Ruth Vanita notes in *Dancing with the Nation: Courtesans in Bombay Cinema*, by the twentieth century, the distinction between a prostitute and a courtesan had blurred. The word 'tawaif' became translucent in its connotation—it could mean either, both. It is this blur that Bhansali uses as narrative ammunition, conveniently making them pillared repositories of culture, and otherwise, pillaged artists dependent on decadent patrons.

The legal definition of the courtesan was first imposed on the imagination by the British and then barrelled down without question or critique into independent India. The Contagious Diseases Act of 1864, passed by the colonial government, brought both courtesans and sex workers under the same bracket, allowing local municipalities the right to relocate them. Convenient, but by no means accurate, the legal imagination was fundamentally incapable of seeing how the courtesans' use of their body differs from that of the sex worker.

The semantic fragility between a 'randi' and a 'tawaif' is best exemplified in the court scene in *Heeramandi*, in which we see Bhansali insist upon a strange and inconsistent manifestation of courtesan culture that somehow makes courtesan culture itself indistinguishable from sex work. Accused of usurping a nawab's property, Mallikajaan is called to the witness box to provide testimony. She describes the work of tawaifs as '*tehzeeb ka mela*', a celebration of politesse, which the lawyer reframes as '*jhoote ishq palna*', cultivating false love—and he isn't wrong. The women of *Heeramandi* do nurture and purr false love.

Mallikajaan tells the lawyer tawaifs are '*pushtaini fankaar*', belonging to a lineage of artists, to counter his invective about the '*jismani taluqat*' or sexual relationships that this art engenders—and here, too, he isn't wrong. He accuses her of buying and selling women—again, he isn't wrong.

Her clinching move is to, instead, make these details seem redundant by pointing out that many an aristocratic lineage survives because of heirs born to tawaifs, often adopted into elite families. This clarifies the trembling distinction between a sex worker and a courtesan that this scene keeps testing. Would a sex worker's blood course through royal bloodlines, it asks without really stating it just so neatly. She, then, asks the nawab's son who gave birth to him, provoking chaos into the order of the courtroom, emerging victorious.

Besides, it is this connotation of 'family', a matrilineal thread of power, that helps distinguish a courtesan from a sex worker. The sense of lineage, a 'celebration of non-marital and non-biological kinship', as Vanita puts it, with a flurry of '*aapas*' and '*khalas*' and '*ammis*', flutters through the story of *Heeramandi*. These are women attempting to fashion a world that does not need men to run it for them, a political lesbianism if you may. Desire for the tawaifs—and this may also be where they mingle with the sex workers of Bhansali's oeuvre—is a wasteland; sex is useless, coded in despair; pleasure is elsewhere.

In *Heeramandi*, set for the most part in a fictional 1940s, Bhansali describes tawaifs as queens of Lahore, bowing to neither patron nor police. It is an entirely ahistorical gaze that refuses to see the courtesan culture as something that was already in steep decline. There is a delusion that is built into the language and posture of the show as it begins, unsure if it belongs to the characters or the makers.

It is this fragile delusion that is both frustrating to see—because it keeps eluding historic and narrative clarity, a steady sense of path and consequence—but also tantalizing. The word 'remanence' comes to mind—the residue, the ability of material to retain its magnetism, long after the removal of the magnetizing field. As Andre Aciman writes, 'Remanence is the memory of something that has vanished and left no trace of itself but that, like a missing limb, continues to exert its presence'[8]. There is something of a vaporous power these women hold, it seems to exist even as it is constantly undermined.

There is also the shameless throwing away of historic accuracy that we are used to in Bhansali's cinema, which makes the fact-finding missions on X (formerly Twitter) feel like it is talking at cross purposes with the show. Some gaffes, though, are unforgivably comical. Urdu scholars on X were exchanging notes on the name of the newspaper Fareedan was reading. No one was able to crack it, until someone realized it was *Tez Hawa*—but written from left to right as separate Urdu letters, *harf-ba-harf*, when it is supposed to be written from right to left. So, if you read it in Urdu, it now says *Aa-o-ha-za-ya-ta*. While it is true that the newspaper Fareedan is reading is bogus, the fact of her reading is essential here. These are learned women, educated and embedded in society.

Throughout Bhansali's *Devdas*, buoyed by Chandramukhi, the tawaif played by Madhuri Dixit, it is clear that she does not belong to civil society. When Parvati (Aishwarya Rai Bachchan) invites her to her haveli for Durga Puja, she has to lie to her family, calling Chandramukhi a 'saheli', her friend from Calcutta. When her identity as a tawaif, a 'bazaru aurat', is outed in front of the zamindars and the villagers, she is humiliated, and from this humiliation emerges her strength—her slap, both verbal and physical. She insists that her work is rendered useful, even plausible by the '*ayyashi*' or decadence of thakurs. There is no mention of the culture they consume as she returns to '*badnaam mohalle ki rangeen raushni*', the colourful light of a tainted mohalla.

In *Heeramandi*, however, the tawaif is considered a respectable figure. Even Qudsia (Farida Jalal), a bleeding heart old aristocratic lady insists that her grandson, Oxford-returned Tajdar (Taha Shah), learn tehzeeb from Heeramandi. She even invites Mallikajaan to their house for a poetry reading. Their presence, their company is not considered tainted; it elevates the aura. For all the high regard Qudsia may accord to Mallikajaan, as a woman from a respectable and elite family, however, Qudsia hasn't ever gone to Heeramandi, and the algebra of 'respectability' is again tampered with. What are the caveats to this respect?

As Bhansali noted in a conversation with Netflix CEO Ted Sarandos, the tawaifs 'lived like queens; they had the nawabs at their beck and call, politicians, British officers. They were artists, connoisseurs of good poetry.' This is the romantic idea of the tawaif as a culture keeper. When he speaks of each individual tawaif character, however, he speaks of 'their angst, their anguish—each one had a story to tell; yet, they were disguising these emotions and coming to the gallery'.

When he focuses on the individual tawaif, it is grief; when it is the collective, it is gemstones. Individual tawaifs have to constantly battle not just the loneliness—'*Iska dil toota hai; ab bani asli tawaif*', now that her heart is broken, she has become a true tawaif—but also the venom flung at them, being called a 'randi' or treated like one, for example. But seen together, spoken of as a community, they are birthplaces of 'tehzeeb'.

It is a rhetorical switch that while pretending to be above the moral demands of its time, also panders to the social reformists of that time. Their work as tawaifs makes them inadequate, and they invariably must evolve, become something else, something nobler. In the end of *Devdas*, Chandramukhi has seen the light, and having learned '*bairaag*' has become a '*jogan*', no longer a tawaif, now a nun to life's pleasures. In *Heeramandi*, the push that all characters experience is, as Bibbojaan says, from 'mujrewali', the one who belongs to the stage, to 'mulkwali', the one who belongs to the country, from a tawaif to a freedom fighter, tying their ghunghroo on staffs that they use as weapons against the police. In both, love lies by the wayside.

While *Heeramandi* takes forward the wretchedness of the tawaif life—films like *Pakeezah* (1972) insisted on hoping for male saviours as virtuous exits—what remains then, are the complicated but adamantine bonds of sisterhood between the tawaifs.

While the connotation of the 'tawaif' is unsteady, it is with the sex worker figure—in *Saawariya*, Gulab, played by Rani Mukerjee, and the women of *Gangubai Kathiawadi*—that Bhansali has absolute clarity. These women are unequivocally rejected by society and hold no pretensions about being on the wrong side of the margins of respectability. Since they are sex workers, they are also brutalized in ways that Chandramukhi never is, because Chandramukhi is a site of tehzeeb, of culture, too.

The sex workers bear their scars from their profession openly, as seen in *Saawariya's* 'Pari'. There is no demand for culture made on the sex workers' body. When they dance, it is not kathak, but the hip thrusting 'Chhabeela', or 'Dholida's' playful garba—the troubling folk versus classical dance distinction.

It might seem from these films that Bhansali's cinema refuses to villainize sex work. In one of the most strident scenes of *Saawariya*, Gulab asks the landlady Lillian, if both of them have things lying empty—Lillian's house, Gulab's body—and so both put them on the market to earn some cash, what, truly distinguishes them? *Gangubai Kathiawadi*, makes a less comical, more social, and also more convoluted case for sex work. Calling it the world's oldest profession, how it is a democratic establishment giving the same rate to everyone irrespective of their place in social hierarchies, Gangubai makes a rousing but strange point that without Kamathipura, the city would turn into a jungle, more women would get raped, families would decimate and '*Hindustani sabhyata*' would fracture. Sex work as a social insurance. So far, so cinematic; delusion as a constant companion.

But it is when the tawaif figure is brought up, that the sex worker figure is demeaned. In *Heeramandi*, the distinction between a 'tawaif' and a 'randi' keeps getting made and ignored, revealing a hierarchy constantly asserted and internalized by the moral compass whose influence clearly extends beyond its characters. When, in *Bajirao Mastani*, Mastani is told to perform for the court, Bajirao blares back, '*Yeh koi nachnewali nahin hai*,' and as such needs to be treated with respect, but the way the word 'nachnewali' is spewed, the connotation is clear—she is pure, unworthy of that profession.

Characters, however, do and say odd things in *Heeramandi* that make the distinction shaky. When

Waheeda propositions the Britisher with her exposed legs, '*Sunne ka shauq nahi toh dekhne ka toh hoga?*', is she acting as an uncultured tawaif or a cultured sex worker?

As Kidwai writes, with the disappearance of real-life tawaifs from our society, the tawaif figure on-screen is emptied of meaning, turned into shape-shifters. Vanita takes this further and argues that attributes of the tawaif figure gets disseminated to non-tawaif characters—serving men alcohol, dancing in public, for example—rendering the tawaif character redundant. Their shapelessness is, perhaps, a consequence of this. But certainly, it is a consequence of Bhansali locating in them, not his allyship, but his desire to gild fractures with beauty. Both the allyship and the gilding require different kinds of care as an artist; the former Bhansali has shown himself entirely incapable of; and the latter, consummately otherwise.

The character of Tajdar (Taha Shah Badussha), son of a nawab, for example, pronounces *Heeramandi* as a place where '*auraton ki izzat ki qeemat lagayi jaati hai*', where their dignity has a price. Crossing lines he falls in love with Alamzeb, the daughter of Mallikajaan. Alamzeb has not yet become a tawaif, and it is the not-yet-ness that makes Tajdar even capable of loving her. With all its renditions of fantasy and delusion, *Heeramandi* does not believe that love is possible in the life of a tawaif. Alamzeb, particularly, becomes a site of this conservative 'purity', such that even her debut mujra is performed in all white—no hips, no cleavage, every inch of skin covered with reams of pleated fabric.

Strangely, even as *Heeramandi* is peppered with double entendres and a shirking comfort with the idea of sex, it is deeply uncomfortable with images of sex. Bibbojaan's nights spent with Henderson or Wali, for example, are merely registered in dialogue, even if the foreplay, the card-flinging and lap-sitting, is available for all to see. But more suspiciously, it is Alamzeb and Tajdar's consummation which happens in an awkward cut between her head on his shoulder and her waking up naked in his bed, only to find herself almost immediately pregnant. Bhansali, even as he articulates his women as erotic figures, is careful to not show them as sexualized beings in *Heeramandi*.

Perhaps, a worry that their association with images of pleasurable or duplicitous sex might render them less courtesan, more sex worker? There is something self-censoring, calculated, and strategic about this omission, a conscious production of sexlessness that in trying to protect the courtesan's image, almost chisels them into sexless beings.

For all that joyful sex and pursuit of pleasure—sexual, literary—*Heeramandi* ends with Alamzeb becoming a tawaif, her inauguration into a world '*jisme kaante biche ho manzil tak*', peppered with thorns, but also achieving the ultimate feminine glory of being a mother. We don't see her practising tawaif-hood because she is young, and youth is a powerfully hopeful thing in Bhansali's cinema. You can ask—why is it that the women in *Saawariya's* 'Pari', the broken sex workers, are all older? Why are the older women in *Heeramandi* offered only full-throated revolution instead of a gut-tickling orgasm? Where are the blooms in *Gangubai Kathiawadi*?

There is something about the tawaif or sex worker figure, invariably older, that is fundamentally tired—romance is not just forgotten but forgiven; there is rarely resentment towards this loss. Some channel this loss into power, some revolution, some reform, and some renunciation. Love is distended into an elsewhere pursuit.

~

Before I take your leave, I want to fixate, a little, on Bhansali's music. While he always had a strong hold over the musical landscape of his films when others composed it—Jatin-Lalit in *Khamoshi: The Musical*, Ismail Darbar in *Hum Dil De Chuke Sanam* and *Devdas*; Monty Sharma in *Saawariya*—he began composing songs himself, first one song for *Saawariya's* album, then full albums, *Guzaarish* onwards. The longer, more elaborate compositions of *Ram-Leela* and *Bajirao Mastani* gave way to the leaner albums of *Padmaavat* and *Gangubai Kathiawadi*.

The word 'jaan', meaning life force, is written in Urdu as 'ja-anh'—the 'anh' as a nasal twang that doesn't allow the tongue to quite touch the roof of the mouth, suspended mid-air, attempting, but not fully able to produce the flatness of the sound 'n'. A strange, stretching, languorous, nasal limbo, it is called *noon ghunna*. Even the script used to give shape to this sound produced the empty, curved ں, like a receptacle whose purpose does not come from merely being, but by being useful, to hold, to store something else.

When Geeta Dutt sings 'Meri Jaan Mujhe Jaan Na Kaho' or when Lata Mangeshkar sings 'Meri Jaan Meri Jaan' or when KK sings 'O Meri Jaan', there is an allegiance to the Urdu language which, when transliterated to Hindi and then romanized into English loses the limbo. Ja-anh often becomes jaan and remains so. (In Urdu, too, this difference is slowly disappearing.)

Tune the ears, then, to how, in the very first song of *Gangubai Kathiawadi*, the singer Neeti Mohan pronounces 'jaan', lending the word its noon ghunna, severing the finality of 'n', bringing in her full-bodied blues, breathing loudly as she arrives at the end of the one-syllable word 'jaan', the saxophones clapping in a funky, rhythmic loop behind her. The shoulders shimmy, the heart sighs.

Her voice loops upwards while singing the word 'nasha', as though walking up a flight of broken, uneven stairs, drunk. Kumar's lyrics are very much a playful ode to not just the fixation in Urdu poetry on the *jaam* and the *paymana*—the glasses and goblets that hold both alcohol and its intoxication—but Bhansali's fixation, too. Alcohol becomes both comfort and catastrophe in *Devdas* and *Heeramandi*, in *Saawariya* it is introduced as that which holds and hides intoxication, the way the body holds and hides the soul—the hero reminds us that like fire in a matchstick, like intoxication in alcohol, the soul, too, isn't visible but why should that mean it doesn't exist? In *Bajirao Mastani* and *Ram-Leela*, it is a sign of emotional tempests; in *Padmaavat*, it is a moral conclusion.

'Meri Jaan' has an atmosphere of unsteady eros, like 'Tilasmi Bahein' also canned in one take, which girds the visuals he spools around it—you don't know which kiss, which insistence becomes charming, then disarming, becomes arrogant, becomes violative. Suddenly, there are horns and percussion, suddenly she yodels, suddenly you can hear her smiling behind the mic, repeating 'Meri Jaan', again and again—thirty times in a barely-four-minute song—like the name of a lover who has pinned you down. This repetition, like a chant, is common throughout the music in Bhansali's cinema, the way '*chaaha*' gets repeated in 'Hamesha Tumko Chaaha' in *Devdas*, like 'Maza Saiba' in *Guzaarish*.

There is a rough around the edges, everything-ness to this song that is both endearing, yet difficult to latch onto because of its amoebic intensity—moving in many directions with the full force of feeling. Bhansali has imagined this song entirely in the back of Gangubai's car as she and her lover wonder, in erotic anticipation, what holds next. Her lover is eager, Gangubai is uncertain, trauma and sadness glazing her eyes, and yet there is that fatal attraction she can't resist. When Bhansali confines his characters in one space, without overt choreography—like the lovers in a room in *Ram-Leela*'s 'Ang Laga De'—the music takes on the heavy lifting. You can hear the sex and pain in the song, the post-coital cigarette being ashed on our erections.

Part of the song's strange effect is its unbound quality, which is the trademark irreverence of Bhansali—towards structure, towards metre. It is the freedom that he gave to his composers, which he expresses through his own music. As Hitesh Sonik, who arranged Bhansali's music in *Guzaarish* notes, 'Gaane ko baandh nahin sakte'[9], that you cannot tie it, pin it down.

The very genre of the song stands as both anachronistic and anatopic—outside of the time and place in which it is being deployed, completely outside the demands of researched realism. In *Heeramandi*, he films 'Nazariya Ki Maari', a mujra—also an ode to Pakeezah, where these very words were strung to another tune, hung in the background of a scene—in an art deco hall with Britishers wearing bracelets of *gajra*, and you can hear in the background of the *thumri* . . . the strum of a guitar. (The guitar strum is in the series, but curiously not in the album) Where are we? Why does it matter?

Then, in gangubai kathiawadi's album, there is 'Dholida', a celebratory song that doesn't need that intensity or improvized intricacy. It needs the throw of a voice, instead, looping in the steady, enamel-like timbre of Jahnvi Shrimankar. On Instagram, as a vote of gratitude, she sang this song without any of the instrumentation, layering, and post-production, and yet that strength is so visible, so confident, so unshaken. Critic Baradwaj Rangan, parsing through the music of Bhansali's films, notes, '[V]oice is always the prime instrument'; never being thrust into the penumbra of a song by the other musical instruments, giving it the dignity of centre stage, '[W]e get the feeling of the songs being sung directly to us.'[10] This might be because so many of his songs are diegetic, characters singing to characters—and often, breaking the fourth wall, to us. While *Heeramandi* is the only album from Bhansali's filmography where every single song is diegetic, performed, lip-synced, his albums are expressions of his characters, even if that isn't verbalized as such by the character themselves.

'Dholida' is visualised as a Bhansali trope we have seen before, in *Ram-Leela*'s 'Nagada Sang Dhol'—celebratory garba where the heroine jousts insouciantly with the dholida, the dhol player, followed by a mournful yet fierce trance. This is not to suggest that Bhansali is running out of ideas as much as he keeps snagging at some recurrent visual and psychological preoccupations, like the woman who is tipped over like a bowling pin by circumstances and music. The musical landscape inherits that transition, then, from contained rhythmic joy to a more scattered devotional chorus of women overlaid by a man flinging his voice at a pitch that feels one *svar,* one note, away from the voice cracking into dust, the tranced woman fallen to the ground in exhaustion.

This gruff, aged, masculine lone voice in a pond of feminine abandon with the full-throated choir and flaring fabrics is a Bhansali invocation that tracks from *Hum Dil De Chuke Sanam*'s 'Nimbooda', *Devdas*' 'Kaahe Chhed Mohe' (Birju Maharaj, here) to 'Deewani Mastani', 'Ghoomar', and now 'Dholida'.

'Jab Saiyan' in *Gangubai Kathiawadi* is Bhansali's first montage song. Alia Bhatt noted in a conversation with Shreya Ghoshal on Instagram, how Bhansali was pacing on set agitated, nervous for he has never done the montage song so apparently in his filmography. Anyone with ideas, he was asking for suggestions.

Bhansali's music is so inextricably woven into his visuals, I have rarely listened to his albums as much as imagined the visuals while listening to them, so pungent is their association. The songs I keep coming back to in my playlist, to just listen to, to while away the day, are songs which Bhansali hasn't bothered giving visuals for—they either never make it to the movie, or are used briefly as connecting tissue, like 'Dhundhli' from *Guzaarish*, 'Laal Ishq' and 'Dhoop' from *Ram-Leela*, 'Aaj Ibaadat' and 'Ab Tohe Jane Na Doongi' from *Bajirao Mastani.* There is a wastefulness here, of songs being pushed into albums that never really get realized on-screen. There is also a piety here, of songs being made for a story, and *only* that story.

The montage song is a test, a tightrope act of the composer's restraint, because the music cannot demand more attention than the visuals for which it is providing an emotional bellwether. Is that why 'Jab Saiyan' croons musically without the gasp, the show, the spectacle of voice? It is pleasant, never sweltering. We are talking of love, aren't we? Unlike the glides between extreme notes, common in Bhansali's music, Shreya Ghoshal inhabits the song with her range that never sounds strained or stretched, moving between the sudden changes in the pace of the song without bringing attention to it—stretching through one syllable, rushing through others.

This song continues Bhansali's invocation of the name of the lover, of the *saiyan*—one that is compared to remembrance in 'Aayat', to perfume and concern and pride in 'Tera Zikr'. His characters scribble the name of the lover on walls across the city, like in *Saawariya* or insist on being called together, not as name and surname but as a hyphenated togetherness—*Ram-Leela*, *Bajirao Mastani*. We rarely title films after characters today because our character names, over the decades, have sponged off their lyrical, suggestive heft. *Gangubai Kathiawadi* continues the older tradition and in 'Jab Saiyan', even attributes the moon-like radiance of Gangubai—established early in the film—to her lover, '*Jab saiyan aaye shaam ko, toh lag gaye chand mere naam ko*,' that when the lover comes back in the evening, it is then my name is elevated, the name being a synecdoche for her being, and 'chand lagna', a metaphor of elevation, of bestowing grace.

For a song filled with soft syllables, A.M. Turaz's sudden sharp lyric 'Chaukhat raukhat' stings the ears. In 'Sau Gram Zindagi', in 'Chand Ki Katori', the sudden slip of English, too, has a similar sting. These are playful ways of going about music, untethered to previously held standards of uncreased crispness and smooth surfaces.

What is fascinating is how, while on the one hand, Bhansali's music allows the vocals to stain past the instrumentation, on the other hand, he allows a free reign to these instruments in patches of musical delight. In 'Jab Saiyan', Bhansali allows for uninterrupted stretches of the sarangi and the harmonium—not as interludes between paragraphs of the 'real' song as it often is employed in A.R. Rahman or Shankar–Ehsan–Loy's compositions. These stretches are often the centrepiece of a song, the emotive anchor, the climax where it crescendos into pulp, like that stretch in 'Lahu Munh Lag Gaya' where the *bhungal*, the Gujarati folk instrument, blares up the scales like a gust of hot wind, or the horns and saxophone of 'Meri Jaan' which has the minty freshness of winking love anticipating a kiss, or what sounds like the mouth organ in 'Tilasmi Baahein', a callback to the sounds of '70s Hindi cinema.

And like an eclectic pit of tunes, from 'Jab Saiyan', we snake through geographies and centuries into the qawwali. Yousuf Saeed, a Delhi-based independent filmmaker and researcher has curated Cinema Qawwali Archive, an online database, according to which, from the birth of the talkies in the early 1930s to 2022, there have been over 800 qawwalis in the movies, 'Shikayat' from *Gangubai Kathiawadi* being the last and latest addition to his archive, as of writing this.

Within cinema, too, we have seen how the qawwali—which comes from qawwal, to posture through speech—has been sown into various shapes, from the techno qawwali of 'Kajra Re' to being mere background music in *Bajrangi Bhaijaan* and *Veer-Zaara* against which the central action of the film takes place.

What was once a musical rendition of Sufi abandon has become something more secular, more accessible, less esoteric. Rahman is, perhaps, one of the few who retain the religious underpinning of the genre. The spiritual heft of Bhansali's qawwali is the longing of a lover.

While there is a lead vocalist (Archana Gore, here, in 'Shikayat') who steers the music, what is novel about the qawwali are the singers in the background who come in as a gale, competing with each other as the song tornadoes towards its crescendo, and then, abruptly claps stop. It is a genre where the chorus is gifted the spotlight, like he did in 'Azadi' in *Heeramandi*.

While melody is important in classical Hindustani, the qawwalis are like an exchange of words put to incidental music—that exchange could be with god, like in 'Kun Faya Kun' from *Rockstar* (2011) or 'Khwaja Mere Khwaja' from *Jodha Akbar* (2008), with a competitor in love like in *Mughal-e-Azam* (1960), just a competitor like in *Shandaar* (2015), or in the case of 'Shikayat', with the lover himself. There is a jostling of voices that takes place, and in 'Shikayat', in one of the most sinuous stretches of music in the album, you can hear a chorus of women cascading down the scales, then jump up the scales, then lower, then pushed up, then lower, as though women, strapped with ghunghroos, are running up and down a proscenium. That playfulness is intact—you can hear it—even as the complaint, the shikayat described by lyricst A.M. Turaz—'*kaleja chahiye khud ko marne ke liye*', the heart is needed to spear it to death—is lodged. To be able to hold both pain and pleasure together.

Kailash Patra's eerie, haunting violin lets us into 'Muskurahat', which like 'Jab Saiyan' is Bhansali bringing us into his rehearsal rooms, as if the melody is still half-formed, as if improvized into being. One of the few remaining music directors who insists on rehearsals, this is where the singer flexes the different dimensions a word can take under a melody. Arijit Singh takes one line, '*Muskurat ko bhi aane de, Mazaa aane lage*' delivering it differently each time—a-a-a-hat, aaa-hat, aa-a-a-a-hat—like this were a classical concert tossing around possibilities as he ravages through a raga; an unstudied, unsteady musicality.

Melisma is central to Bhansali's sense of music, as has been pointed out by Rangan—where usually one syllable is assigned one svar, Bhansali packs a syllable with as many svars as he can, a greed but also a desire to produce a musical density. 'Jab Saiyan' doesn't leave a syllable without pummelling it with melody. Here, too, train your ears to the aa in 'muskurane' or in 'nasha' or the 'i' in 'khushi'—when he sees a vowel, he tests its tensile, musical malleability. How much can it be stretched? How much music can a sound produce? Then, smack in the middle of the song is a moment of complete silence.

And before the album sends us packing off, and I send you packing off, a folk song, 'Jhume Re Gori', like 'Mor Bani Thangat' or 'Bhai Bhai' in *Ram-Leela*, like bridging what is considered 'classical' with what is considered, by those who perform classical, 'folk'—the merriment of folk, the sobriety of classical are categories that Bhansali, to his detriment, deepens in his albums, even as he brings them in conversation by placing them in the same film, shoulder to shoulder. If there is 'Albela Sajan' in *Hum Dil De Chuke Sanam* in Raag Ahir-Bhairav, there is also the kite-flying communal ripple 'Kaipoche'.

Bhansali's artistry isn't stuck in amber, that much is clear. He will bring in the popular Arijit Singh but make his voice unrecognizable, as he did in 'Bint-e-dil' in *Padmaavat*. Even if he gives you a pale Shreya Ghoshal, he will throw in new artists, new sounds, a new way of thinking of the *virah* song, the song of separation, as not something that can be sung easily, replicated, re-sung, re-mixed across the cultural landscape, but must be soaked in.

While relishing his influences—Lata Mangeshkar, K. Asif, V. Shantaram, Guru Dutt, R.D. Burman—he is never bound by his reverence, allowing for instinct to triumph. If the instinct is bluesy, then so be it. If the instinct is Arijit skating the highest pitch, in what Bhansali imagines as 'oriental', while most composers would be content with Arijit merely breathing through words, then so be it. Who gives their heavily accented Gujarati protagonist a bluesy erotic song, a dholida to squirm in the streets with her gang, and a song that reaches back to the annals of Urdu poetry?

After producing three musical paragons of what an album should sound like—*Guzaarish*, *Ram-Leela*, and *Bajirao Mastani*—even if they were wasteful, Bhansali is now producing leaner albums, or perhaps musically leaner films. Just six songs, clocking in under twenty-three minutes, the songs of *Gangubai Kathiawadi* move quickly between genres of feeling. With nine songs, the album of *Heeramandi* is a crisp half-hour, with songs merely stating their purpose, before their farewell—quick songs. Besides, the songs are not as tied to characters, their poetry has an ambiguity that can be slipped around between characters. In fact, some actors were asked which thumri they would want to perform to.

You cannot listen to these albums as a single mood piece neatly transitioning, like you would for his longer albums. Both *Ram-Leela* and *Bajirao Mastani*, for example, were released as jukeboxes on YouTube in two parts, each with a separate personality. The swerves in *Gangubai Kathiawadi's* album are sudden, the jolts more conspicuous, the genres more distinct. As if the songs don't belong in the same universe, a patchwork quilt yanked together forcefully by Bhansali's rapacious appetite for that which rips us out beyond our being, that much beauty.

As *Gangubai Kathiawadi* fades into its runtime, with each of her adversities and adversaries sated and stumbled—the greedy kothewali replaced, the local rapist bludgeoned, the local politician crumpled into defeat, the local school protesting their brothel silenced, with a visit to Nehru to convince him of sex workers' humanity—shaking with a triumphant glow, we see her celebrated as a figure, one who, nonetheless, like Michelle McNellie in *Black*, is alone at the end, on her pedestal.

She joins the caravan of Bhansali's broken hearts—the tawaifs of *Heeramandi*, Samir in Italy from *Hum Dil De Chuke Sanam* watching Nandini recede, Ranbir Raj from *Saawariya* watching Sakina vaporize into her other life, Paro in colonial Bengal and Kashibai in Maratha Wai, mourning the death of Devdas and Bajirao respectively, men who loved them, but have loved elsewhere, too.

In Conclusion

Tum to gaye par yaad na gayi
Zubaan se meri faryaad naa gayi

You might have gone
But my memory remained,
My complaint has not ceded

—A. M. Turaz

Maybe the worst place to explain the thrust of your book, the seething intention behind its words, is the conclusion, and maybe I am the worst in doing so, and so be it.

The Canadian artist Agnes Martin was visited by a friend and the friend's granddaughter. Out of a vase of roses, Martin plucked one, placing the fragrant flower in front of the granddaughter, asking if she found the rose beautiful. The young girl replied, yes. Martin then hid the rose behind her back, and asked if the rose was still beautiful, to which the young girl again replied in the affirmative, that, yes, the rose was still beautiful.

Martin clinched this exchange, spinning this reaction into an anecdote, telling the young girl, you see, beauty lies not in the object, but in the mind that perceives it, in the mind that remembers it, and the mind that reproduces this memory.

I tell this story, because sometimes I feel, with films like *Saawariya*, their beauty burns brighter in my memory of them than in my viewing of them. There is, simply, no way to know.

I had first heard *Saawariya* before I watched it. After the Diwali holidays, a school friend, my bus companion, came hurried, breathless, to tell me of this strange movie he saw, it was all blue and nothing really made sense. A line about the grumpy landlady Lillian (Zohra Segal, in her last performance) turning people she doesn't like to 'chicken tandoori', he interpreted literally, and the film gained a strange Marquez-like glint in my head. Magic realism, however, was too weak a phrase to describe what Bhansali did to cinema with *Saawariya*, requiring not just suspension, but a renunciation of disbelief, a rewiring of all the things I considered essential to 'good' cinema.

In that bus, my friend went ahead describing the film scene by scene, as accurately as he could remember it, which I force-fit into the images from the film floating as trailers and teasers on television. Slowly, something was building in my head. I knew I loved it, even as he described what he saw with what bordered on distaste, but which on children often sounds like confounded boredom. I had to merely confirm this love, which I did, later, at the movies.

Perhaps, then, instead of questioning the myth, I am scratching at it in this book, trying to edify an intuition.

The films I have chosen to fixate on in this monograph and the intensity of the fixation is testament to this sparking.

Later, when browsing the theatres as my parents and I did regularly in the weekends, I chanced upon a poster of *Guzaarish*, of Aishwarya Rai Bachchan holding Hrithik Roshan in her arms, an expression of pain on her face and relief on his, and I stood there, unknowing of the aesthetic 'affinity' that was bubbling within me—all of fourteen-years-old—until I was yanked back into the theatre for the film we came for was beginning. By 'affinity' I mean what Brian Dillon meant, 'a realm of the unthought, unthinkable, something unkillable by attitudes or arguments . . . Something fleeting, in fact . . . Something a little bit stupid.'

You might have sensed in my language this urgency, a gripping desperation with which I cling to Bhansali's filmography. To see contemporary Hindi cinema blur by, as we critics do, shoved into one or two or three preview screenings every week, is to experience, at best, an agnosticism around beauty.

It is not that these filmmakers don't believe in beauty. Neither is it that they, like say director Mrinal Sen, are consciously pursuing ugliness, where to keep his socially grounded movies intact, 'it [was] very important to [him] to make things look unpretty, to keep the rough edges.' It is that they are lulling somewhere between not believing and not pursuing it—they are not even considering it. There is a frustrating ambivalence, as though beauty weren't an apparent, even necessary part of cinema. For me, then, a kind of person who finds beauty as essential to life as ethics—don't shriek, please—cinema, too, must uphold certain standards of not just narrative and character, but beauty, too.

This ambivalence, perhaps, is rooted in the careless yet calibrated way cinema is conceived of in the 'industry', as a 'product'. When, in October 2022, to celebrate the forty-five years Vidhu Vinod Chopra spent in the movies, there was a re-run of his films—*Sazaye Maut* (1981), *Khamosh* (1985), *Parinda* (1989), *1942: A Love Story* (1994), *Mission Kashmir* (2000), and *Eklavya: The Royal Guard* (2007), among other films that Chopra produced—this desperation was put back in perspective.

Bhansali worked with Chopra on both *Parinda* and *1942: A Love Story*. For the former he was 'Associate Director—Songs'. And in the latter, when he started using his middle name 'Leela', he was credited for both 'Screenplay' and 'Director—Songs'. It was attached to music, his legacy in cinema

Seeing the textured, bird-flecked Bombay of *Parinda*, the fluttering, silken visuals of *1942: A Love Story's* songs come to life on the big screen—what joy to watch cinema that pays such attention to the surface, its polish, its contrasts, shapes, sounds, winds, its tinted glory.

On the other hand, and this is where, somewhere, I hope my words puncture, I am wary of how 'Bhansali' has been promoted, in the cultural lexicon, from noun to adjective. Any image, any film with the slightest hint of exaggeration, of grandiosity, of intentional exuberance, is described as being made in the shadow of Bhansali.

Bhansali cinema—as opposed to Bhansali's cinema—is not just the cinema of Bhansali, but cinema like Bhansali's. This book is, then, also, a vigorous attempt at nouning his cinema back to him, by invasively watching what makes his artistic practice so specific and inimitable. Sometimes you see him straying. In *Heeramandi*, for instance, every mujra was cut away from, only to return to it after a scene, or letting it sigh into its premature demise. This kind of disregard for the song is new, this kind of regard for narrative is new. You almost wish he did not get distracted by the story. Even if he does not return to his cinema, and its back-breaking demands on drama and beauty—both easy and uneasy beauty—at least *we* can return, if not through spectatorship, then through words, through memory. This is that.

Acknowledgements

To celebrate twenty-five years of Bhansali in the movies, in 2023, at Film Companion we produced a labour of love—a webpage 'A-Z of Sanjay Leela Bhansali' that takes you through his filmography, his vision, and his reputation. Mohini Chaudhuri, who was then the Managing Editor, and I spent months speaking to as many of his collaborators as we could and put the page together. That was the seed from which this book emerged. Without Mohini's vision and tenacity, I do not think that page would have happened, and if that page would not have happened, I am unsure of this book's existence.

Months later, I walked into the office of Anupama Chopra, founder and editor of Film Companion, asking her why no one in India is writing trade books about filmographies—not filmmakers about whom mediocre biographies abound, not "making of" books on iconic films, but writing about films as objects and journeys unto themselves. Where are the monographs? She sent out emails, got me represented by an agency, and here we are.

Without her generosity, her kindness, and her persistence, this book would have remained an idea, and without Film Companion . . . I shudder to even pull that thought further.

Without Deepanjana Pal, under whose exacting but edifying editorship (she is probably rolling her eyes at the alliteration) I was writing at Film Companion, I would not have found the time to turn this idea into a book.

Ambar Sahil Chatterjee at 'A Suitable Agency' understood with clarity and rigour that is almost infectious, from the very first email, what I wanted to write, how I wanted to write it, and he refused to make me doubt myself. Thank you, Hemali Sodhi, for taking me on.

Chirag Thakkar, who brought me onto Penguin Random House, believed in not just my craft, but the book, too, sharpening the demands (he made me write more, when I thought I had less to say), doing his best to set me up for success. Thank you. Anushree Kaushal, Angelin Joy and Aninda Das at Penguin Random House, for combing through the manuscript with attention and care, thank you.

Suchin Mehrotra, Kush Patel, Azraa Ismail, Shivani Bhasin, Tanvi Ajinkya, Akshita Wadhwana, may friends be as you are—kind, giving, and patient. To uncritically love, I have learned from you. You read my manuscript, you spoke of me with pride, that is enough.

Baradwaj Rangan, for bringing film criticism into my life, and later, bringing my life into film criticism. You make this profession look possible. Nasreen Munni Kabir, for telling me to sharpen my thoughts, clarify my language, and express my love with caution, thank you for your thoughts, and for your words—a roadmap for anyone thinking of film writing.

Chitti, Chittappa, Kaavya, Paati, for making Mumbai possible, for making Mumbai home, thank you.

Amma for never saying no to movies and appa for never saying no to books—you led me here. And since you both will insist, thank you god.

Notes

Introduction

1 Rahul Bhatia, 'The Curious Case of Saawariya', *Open* magazine, 14 April 2010. https://openthemagazine.com/features/business/the-curious-case-of-saawariya/ [Retrieved 13 December 2023]
2 Rajeev Masand, 'Saawariya Fails To Strike A Chord', November 2007
3 Rahul Bhatia, 'The Curious Case of Saawariya', *Open* magazine, 14 April 2010. https://openthemagazine.com/features/business/the-curious-case-of-saawariya/ [Retrieved 13 December 2023]
4 Swarup Chakraborty, 'Hollywood studios' track record in India patchy', *Business Standard*, 21 January, 2013. https://www.business-standard.com/article/companies/hollywood-studios-track-record-in-india-patchy-110060800078_1.html [Retrieved 14 March 2024]
5 Nisha Susan, 'My grandmother sold a silver thali and bought us a plastic pigeon', *Tehelka*, 29 October 2011. http://old.tehelka.com/my-grandmother-sold-a-silver-thali-and-bought-us-a-plastic-pigeon/ [Retrieved 14 January 2024]

6 Richard Brody, 'Earth Mama' Reinvigorates the Closeup, the Beating Heart of the Cinema', *New Yorker*, 13 July 2023. https://www.newyorker.com/culture/the-front-row/earth-mama-reinvigorates-the-closeup-the-beating-heart-of-the-cinema [Retrieved 13 December 2023]
7 'I felt like a vagina: Swara Bhaskar slams Sanjay Leela Bhansali in scathing open letter against Padmaavat', *Hindustan Times*, 29 January 2018. https://www.hindustantimes.com/bollywood/i-felt-like-a-vagina-swara-bhaskar-slams-sanjay-leela-bhansali-in-scathing-open-letter-against-padmaavat/story-1OBBnoBcwHQIwouTJwCFgM.html [Retrieved 20 August 2024]
8 Priya Gupta, 'When I am not being watched, I too am a loud Gujarati: Sanjay Leela Bhansali', *Times Of India*, 12 November 2013. https://timesofindia.indiatimes.com/entertainment/hindi/bollywood/news/sanjay-leela-bhansali-hum-dil-de-chuke-sanam-saraswatichandra/articleshow/25591828.cms [Retrieved 13 December 2023]
9 Bence Nanay, *Aesthetics: A Very Short Introduction* Oxford University Press, 2019.
10 Shahida Bari, 'The puzzle of beauty', Aeon.co, 7 May 2018. https://aeon.co/essays/what-is-beauty-if-not-a-jolt-that-awakens-us-to-the-world [Retrieved 13 December 2023]
11 B.N. Goswamy, *The Spirit of Indian Painting*, Allen Lane India, 2015.
12 Ziya Us Salam, *Being Muslim in Hindu India*, HarperCollins, 2023.
13 Sebastian Smee, 'The artist who rewrote the rules', *Telegraph*, 17 March 2004. https://www.telegraph.co.uk/culture/3613943/The-artist-who-rewrote-the-rules.html [Retrieved on 27 March 2024]
14 Sebastian Smee, 'Beauty review – so much for the pleasures of the flesh', *Guardian*, 22 March 2009. https://www.theguardian.com/books/2009/mar/21/beauty-roger-scruton-art-books [Retrieved on 13 December 2023]

15 Priyadarshi Patnaik, 'Rasa Aesthetics Goes Global', *The Bloomsbury Research Handbook of Indian Aesthetics and the Philosophy of Art* (Ed: Arindam Chakrabarti), 2022.

Chapter 1: Seeds Sown in *Khamoshi: The Musical*

1 https://www.facebook.com/watch/?v=363086968469617
2 Uday Bhatia, '*Bullets Over Bombay*', Harper Collins, 2021.
3 Mihika Agarwal, 'The dying single-screen theatres of India are taking with them her cultural heritage', *Architectural Digest*, 5 August 2022. https://www.architecturaldigest.in/story/the-dying-single-screen-theaters-of-india-are-taking-with-them-her-cultural-heritage/ [Retrieved 23 January 2024]
4 Damient Walters, 'The great escape', Aeon, 12 July 2013. https://aeon.co/essays/does-fantasy-offer-mere-escapism-or-real-escape [Retrieved 25 December 2023]
5 YouTube, "FTF Sanjay Leela Bhansali 17 7 2002", 23 January 2012. https://www.youtube.com/watch?v=YXJAiLJ3WK4 [Retrieved on 20 August 2024]
6 'The History and Practice of Cinematography in India: Anil Mehta', Raqs Media Collective. https://works.raqsmediacollective.net/wp-content/uploads/2022/11/anil_mehta-2.pdf [Retireved 23 January 2024]

Chapter 2: Darshan in *Devdas*

1 WildFilmsIndia, 'Sanjay Leela Bhansali on working with Shahrukh, Madhuri Dixit and Aishwarya in Devdas', YouTube, 22 February 2022. https://www.youtube.com/watch?v=laynCJRyIn8&t=11s&ab_channel=WildFilmsIndia [Retrieved 23 January 2024]
2 Ibid.
3 Sheela Raval, Anupama Chopra, 'Devdas: How Sanjay Leela Bhansali's gamble paid off', *India Today*, 2002. https://www.indiatoday.in/india-today-insight/story/from-the-

archives-2002-devdas-how-sanjay-leela-bhansali-s-gamble-paid-off-1975155-2022-07-13 [Retrieved 17 March 2024]

4 Arundhathi Subramaniam, 'Dance in Films', MARG Magazine, 2003.

5 'Rowdy Rathore has put me in a happy positive frame of mind: Sanjay Leela Bhansali', Hindustan Times, 11 June 2012. https://www.hindustantimes.com/bollywood/rowdy-rathore-has-put-me-in-a-happy-positive-frame-of-mind-sanjay-leela-bhansali/story-svkLqrCz6vqtD1HhMyKv1H.html [Retrieved 20 August 2024]

6 Anupama Chopra, 'Devdas: How Sanjay Leela Bhansali's gamble paid off', India Today, 2002. https://www.indiatoday.in/india-today-insight/story/from-the-archives-2002-devdas-how-sanjay-leela-bhansali-s-gamble-paid-off-1975155-2022-07-13 [Retrieved 23 January 2024]

7 Leo Robson, 'No Connection', New Left Review, 29 October 2021. https://newleftreview.org/sidecar/posts/no-connection [Retrieved 23 January 2024]

8 'The Team Behind Khamoshi Recalls How Sanjay Bhansali's First Film Got Made', Cinestaan, 9 August 2016. https://www.cinestaan.com/articles/2016/aug/9/1663/the-team-behind-khamoshi-recalls-how-sanjay-bhansali-s-first-film-got-made [Retireved 20 September 2023]

Chapter 3: *Saawariya*, Doused in Blues

1 Roland Barthes, translated by Richard Howard, '*A Lover's Discourse*', 1977.

2 Gillian Rose, '*Love's Work*', NYRB Classics, 2011.

3 Amit Chaudhuri, '*Finding the Raga: An Improvisation on Indian Music*', Penguin Hamish Hamilton, 2021.

4 Michiel Baas, '*Muscular India: Masculinity, Mobility & The New Middle Class*', Context, 2020.

5 Shannon Philip, 'Becoming Young Men in a New India: Masculinities, Gender Relations and Violence in the Postcolony', Cambridge University Press, 2022.

6 Filmer Films, 'SAAWARIYA - IN THE MAKING with RANBIR KAPOOR, SONAM KAPOOR and SANJAY LEELA BHANSALI', YouTube, 13 June 2020. https://www.youtube.com/watch?v=FsqJ-c3ISeI&ab_channel=FILMERFILMS [Retrieved 24 January 2024]
7 Edmund Burke, '*A Philosophical Enquiry into the Origins of the Sublime and Beautiful*', 1757.
8 Jessica Frazier, 'Ancient Indian texts reveal the liberating power of metaphysics', Psyche.co, 15 February 2022. https://psyche.co/ideas/ancient-indian-texts-reveal-the-liberating-power-of-metaphysics [Retrieved 3 Jan 2024]
9 Rishi Kapoor with Meena Iyer, '*Khullam Khulla*', Harper Collins, 2017.
10 Anand Pandian, '*Reel World: On Location in Kollywood*', Penguin Books Limited, 27 January 2017.
11 Sergei Eisenstein, '*Towards a Theory of Montage*', 1994, British Film Institute.
12 'Mark Rothko: Early Career (1903 – 1948)', National Gallery of Art. https://www.nga.gov/features/mark-rothko/mark-rothko-early-years.html [Retrieved 20 August 2024]
13 George Kouvaros & Lesley Stern, '*Falling for You: Essays on Cinema and Performance*', University of Sydney, 2000.
14 Usha Iyer, 'The Many Bodies of the Dancer-Actress: Towards A Kinesics of Film Acting', *The Oxford Handbook of Film Theory*, 2022.

Chapter 4: Violence in Beauty, Violence as Beauty in *Ram-Leela*

1 https://www.poetryfoundation.org/articles/69400/tradition-and-the-individual-talent
2 https://thepointmag.com/criticism/negative-criticism/
3 Baradwaj Rangan, 'Ravi K. Chandran Interview With Baradwaj Rangan | Part 2 | Masterclass | Saawariya | Black', Film Companion, 26 August 2021. https://www.youtube.com/watch?v=br2ow6mAxG8&ab_channel=FilmCompanionSouth [Retrieved 28 January 2024]

4 Sebastian Smee, 'This dashing self-portrait by Rembrandt is one of his greatest', Washington Post, 8 April 2022. https://www.washingtonpost.com/arts-entertainment/interactive/2022/rembrandt-self-portrait/ [Retrieved 27 January 2024]
5 C. Fuentes, 'The Novel as Tragedy: William Faulkner', 1995.
6 https://x.com/peligrietzer/status/1734178300036030610 [Retrieved on 20 August 2024]
7 Damini Purkayastha, 'Being Sophia, Aishwarya style', Hindustan Times, 20 November 2010. https://www.hindustantimes.com/entertainment/being-sophia-aishwarya-style/story-QpQ1XgubyqtlCsMY6ZlZ4K.html
8 Daniel J. Walkin, 'Bollywood Flavors Opening of Spoleto', New York Times, 28 June 2008. https://www.nytimes.com/2008/06/28/arts/music/28fest.html [Retrieved 27 January 2024]
9 Andrew Clements, 'Padmâvatî', The Guardian, 19 March 2008. https://www.theguardian.com/music/2008/mar/19/classicalmusicandopera1 [Retrieved 20 August 2024]
10 'Sanjay Leela Bhansali Interview with Anupama Chopra | Director's Cut | Film Companion', YouTube, 14 January 2019. https://www.youtube.com/watch?v=HIe53wJGYhM [Retrieved 20 August 2024]

Chapter 5: Other Kinds of Beauty in *Gangubai Kathiawadi*

1 Prathyush Parasuraman, 'Breaking Down Alia Bhatt's All-White Costumes Of Gangubai Kathiawadi', Film Companion, 3rd March 2022. https://www.filmcompanion.in/interviews/gangubai-kathiawadi-alia-bhatt-sanjay-leela-bhansali-breaking-down-all-white-costumes [Retrieved 20 August 2024]
2 Amit Chaudhuri, 'The restiveness of Asha', India Seminar, 2021. https://www.india-seminar.com/2021/741/741_amit_chaudhuri.htm [Retrieved 28 January 2024]
3 Ruth Vanita, '*Dancing with the Nation: Courtesans in Bombay Cinema*', Speaking Tiger, 2017.

4 Mayank Austen Soofi, '*Nobody Can Love You More: Life in Delhi's Red Light District*', Penguin India, 2012.
5 Aditya Vikram, 'The Talk Of The Heart, It's Not As Easy As It Looks' : Saleem Kidwai's Friendship with Begum Akhtar', Agents Of Ishq, 12 September 2021. https://agentsofishq.com/post/saleem-kidwais-friendship-with-begum-akhtar [Retrieved 8 January 2023]
6 Vikram Phukan, 'The Enduring Queer Appeal of Lata Mangeshkar', 23 September 2011. https://vikramphukan.wordpress.com/2011/09/23/shes-singing-our-song/ [Retrieved 8 January 2023]
7 Shruti Janardhan, 'Madhavi Menon Wants Us To Embrace Ambiguity', Verve, 17 March 2022. https://www.vervemagazine.in/people/madhavi-menon-wants-us-to-embrace-ambiguity [Retrieved 8 January 2023]
8 Andre Aciman, '*Homo Irrealis*', Farrar, Straus and Giroux, 2021.
9 UTV Motion Pictures, 'Guzaarish - Musical Dream In Making', YouTube, 11 November 2010. https://www.youtube.com/watch?v=xB97qtZMZtU&t=481s&ab_channel=UTVMotionPictures [Retrieved 13 December 2023]
10 Baradwaj Rangan, 'Songs Of The Soul', Wordpress, 6 November 2010. https://baradwajrangan.wordpress.com/2010/11/06/between-reviews-6/ [Retrieved 13 December 2023]

Scan QR code to access the
Penguin Random House India website